Pathways to Understanding:

Patterns and Practices in the Learning-Focused Classroom

by
Laura Lipton and Bruce Wellman

Foreword by Arthur L. Costa

Layout and Cover Design: Michael Buckley

Third Edition
MiraVia, LLC Sherman CT

Pathways to Understanding:

Patterns and Practices in the Learning-Focused Classroom

by
Laura Lipton and Bruce Wellman

MiraVia, LLC, 3 Lost Acre Trail, Sherman CT 06784
www.miravia.com

Copyright © 1998 by Laura Lipton and Bruce Wellman
First Printing June 1998
Second Printing January 1999
Third Printing May 2000
Fourth Printing November 2001
Fifth Printing October 2002
Sixth Printing July 2004
Seventh Printing July 2006
Printed in the United States of America

ISBN 0-9665022-0-5   Softcover

Table of Contents

Foreword

Thinking is an engagement of the mind that changes the mind.
　　　　　　　　　　　　　　　　　　　　—Martin Heiddegar

If you view learners as capable, creative and cognitive, if you view yourself as a facilitator rather than a director of learning, if you believe that the act of learning should be joyful—even euphoric—and if you hold the belief that the intent of education is not only for knowledge acquisition but for knowledge production, then . . . read on!

The orientation of this book is that meaning-making is not a spectator sport. Knowledge is a constructive process rather than a finding; it is not the content stored in memory but the processes of constructing it that gets stored. Humans don't *get* ideas; they *make* ideas.

Drawing on years of research and experience, Laura Lipton and Bruce Wellman have gathered, invented and organized a vast treasure of instructional techniques, strategies and tools based on a three-phase framework intended to engage, activate and transform the mind. This book is also a statement of Bruce and Laura's philosophical beliefs and values. When you apply their powerful strategies, you will be exemplifying and manifesting a set of beliefs about how human beings learn most effectively. Anyone who serves others—children and adults—with the intent of learning will find this book to be an essential resource.

Bruce and Laura view teachers as mediators of self-directed learning. In this role, the teacher interposes him- or herself between the learner and the learning, causing students to approach events, tasks and problems strategically, monitoring their own progress, constructing meaning from their experiences and applying their learnings to other contexts and settings. Purposefully applying the activities in this book assures that students are fully engaged in the processes of meaning-making. Instruction is organized so that students are the producers of their own knowledge rather than consumers of someone else's knowledge.

In this volume, Bruce and Laura offer a template for mediational questions and a format for problems to be posed which will stimulate the brain, challenge increasingly more complex intellectual capacities and activate creative potentials. These methods provide students with perplexing situations, intriguing discrepancies, and metaphorical tasks—the resolution of which are not readily apparent and therefore must be designed and constructed. During and after activity, participants are invited to reflect on their thinking and to make meaning from their experiences—to compare intended with actual outcomes, to analyze and draw causal relationships, to synthesize meanings and to apply their learnings to new and novel situations.

Learning requires experimentation, and to experiment, the classroom environment must be safe. Bruce and Laura envision classrooms where there are no failures or mistakes—only learning from experience. Inviting self-evaluation and providing non-judgmental feedback encourages students to pursue their ideas deeply and courageously, developing the capacity for judging the worth of their own ideas. Listening to, paraphrasing, clarifying, and pursuing students' thoughts conveys your belief that their minds have the power to produce meaningful concepts.

The authors view learning as a reciprocal process: the individual influences the group and the group influences the individual. Learners construct meaning interactively. While meaning-making may be an individual experience, the social processes of interaction and participation produce perceptual richness which enhances and refines those meanings.

What are the benefits of implementing this approach? The payoff will be found in the brightness of learners' eyes, the excitement of their self-discovery, the exuberance of their participation, the enhancement of their self-esteem, their intrigue with the mysterious and their joyous expressions of insight. Furthermore, when you assume the identity of a mediator and devote your energies to serving other's construction of meaning, a profound transformation in your own thoughts and values occurs. You find enormous power within yourself to positively influence others and you gain personal satisfaction in using your talents to enhance their achievement. You expand your repertoire of instructional strategies and you will soon find yourself applying this view of learning in a variety of life-situations beyond the classroom. You will embark, along with those you teach, on a magical journey of continuous and lifelong learning. After all, isn't that what being a teacher is all about?

Arthur L. Costa, Ed. D
Kalaheo, Hawaii

Acknowledgments

As colleagues and co-learners we have explored the terrain of meaning-making for more than ten years, continually making meaning through shared adventures and new discoveries along the way. This book represents one branch of our pathway to understanding.

Many valued others have been part of our journey. Some have blazed a trail before us, providing guideposts to mark the way, others have walked along with us, sharing their observations and illuminating our thinking. This work gives us an opportunity to express our respect and regard to these teachers and co-learners.

Our thanks to Arthur Costa, Luan Felleman, Robin Fogarty, Robert Garmston, Mary Ann Haley, David Hyerle, Joyce Juntune, Carolee Matsumoto, Mary Budd Rowe, Jon Saphier, Diane Zimmerman as well as countless colleagues past and present from whom we have learned and with whom we have grown.

We have also had the remarkable experiences of teaching and learning with hundreds of classroom teachers throughout the United States, Canada, Europe, New Zealand and Australia. These generous practitioners have shared their thinking and challenged ours in seminars and workshops; invited us into their classrooms; and offered us samples of their instructional repertoire and student products.

As a tangible product of our imaginations, experiences and learning, the original production of this book would not have been possible without Nancy Morrissey, who provided flexibility, detail-orientation and an unfailing sense of humor. We also offer our most sincere appreciation to Michael Buckley for extending his sound advice, guidance and hands-on production support in lay-out and design. He has vastly improved our graphic literacy.

About the Authors

Laura Lipton, Ed.D, is Co-Director of *MiraVia, LLC* (Sherman, CT). She is an instructional strategist who specializes in curriculum and instructional design to promote thinking, learning and thoughtful assessment. Her broad teaching background includes K-12 general and special education and teacher preparation courses. Dr. Lipton has extensive experience in integrating curriculum, literacy development, building thinking skills, thoughtful assessment and cultivating collaborative cultures. She leads workshops and seminars throughout the United States, Canada, Europe, Australia and New Zealand.

Laura can be contacted at:
3 Lost Acre Trail • Sherman, CT • 06784
P. 860-354-4543 • F. 860-354-6740 • e-mail: lelipton@miravia.com

Bruce Wellman, M.Ed, is Co-Director of *MiraVia, LLC*. (Sherman, CT). He consults with school systems, professional groups and publishers throughout the United States and Canada, presenting workshops and courses for teachers and administrators on teaching methods and materials, thinking skills development, mentoring beginning teachers, presentation skills and facilitating collaborative groups. Mr. Wellman has served as a classroom teacher, curriculum coordinator and staff developer in the Oberlin, Ohio, and Concord, Massachusetts, public schools. He holds a B.A. degree from Antioch College and an M.Ed from Lesley College.

Bruce can be contacted at:
229 Colyer Road • Guilford, VT • 05301
P. 802-257-4892 • F. 802-257-2403 • e-mail: bwellman@miravia.com

PATHWAYS TO UNDERSTANDING: An Introduction

IDEAL *teachers are individuals who see themselves as bridges over which students can cross, then, having facilitated their crossing, joyfully collapse, encouraging them to create their own bridges.*

—Kazantzakis

Pathways to Understanding

In Carol Barrmann's second grade classroom in Hyde Park, New York, students work in cooperative groups to sort animal picture cards into categories. She directs them to "group the cards in any way that makes sense to everyone on your team" and tells them, "I'll be choosing someone to explain the team's thinking, so be sure everyone is ready to discuss your categories." After ten minutes of group work, the chosen reporters stay at their tables while the remainder of each cooperative group rotates to each of the other tables. They view and discuss their fellow students' work in five-minute intervals, switching tables at Carol's signal. Returning to their original table, students have the opportunity to review and refine their groupings, adding new thoughts and ideas gleaned from their classmates.

"I'm comparing Willie Wonka with Abraham Lincoln." "What are some ways that Anastasia is like Madonna?" In El Paso, Texas, students in Mark Stevens' sixth grade Language Arts class have been asked to choose a fictional character from any of the literature that they have read this year and create a Venn diagram comparing that character to someone making news today. They enthusiastically engage with each other and the information as they consider ideas and possibilities. Then students begin their own graphic organizer.

"Analyze the class activity about the number line. What worked for you, what did not? What did it help to clarify; what is still not clear?" In Cumberland County, North Carolina, Carol Lloyd's ninth grade algebra students are responding to this question in their math journals. Carol's students are asked to respond in their journals twice weekly. Other questions ask them to explain the way(s) in which they derived an answer to a problem; to evaluate their answer or product based on specific criteria; to describe how they solved a problem, and think of at least two alternative methods for solving the same problem. Carol reviews their journals every three weeks. She often gets pictures, and sometimes even poems, as journal entries.

The three classrooms described here span diverse geographical regions, grade levels and content areas. Yet they all have a great deal in common. The instructional activities, materials and learning environment established by each teacher is based upon the most current research on teaching and learning. This body of research indicates that when learners consciously employ strategies to organize and integrate information, they enhance their learning, increase retention of knowledge and skills and transfer this learning to other settings. More importantly, use of learning strategies, which characterizes successful students, can be taught to those students who have been less successful in learning situations. In fact, explicit strategy instruction, coupled with diverse opportunities for practice, specific and immediate feedback and application to novel situations can dramatically improve the performance of low achieving students. Given these conditions, all students can become skilled learners and problem solvers with a higher likelihood of success in school and success in life.

The common elements of effective practice illustrated by these dynamic classrooms offers implications for learning-focused practice. This book explores pathways to understanding; pathways that teachers and students can travel together to discover the connections that make learning meaningful. As you explore this volume, you'll find a dynamic, research-based model for instruction designed to promote greater learning for all students. The principles and patterns of learning-focused environments will be illuminated by specific and practical strategies for immediate application to your own work.

New Vistas, New Ventures

Chapter One is organized around eight powerful patterns for learning. These principles for practice establish a research-based context for learning-focused classrooms.

Chapter Two introduces and describes a teaching/learning cycle which serves as a template for effective, interactive instructional design. This model, a foundation for learning-focused classrooms, translates theory into practice with relevance and accessibility.

Chapter Three provides key information and practical ideas for verbal and nonverbal classroom discourse designed to challenge thinking, and foster problem-solving and decision-making skills.

Chapter Four lays out a continuum of interaction patterns for establishing high engagement and high interest. From simple paired activities to elaborately designed cooperative structures, this chapter guides positive, productive student interaction.

Chapter Five is an explorer's backpack; organized to provide support, resources and sustenance for your journey. As you travel through the book, watch for the **A** indicating that a blackline master can be found in Chapter 5.

This book is filled with a rich array of strategies and suggestions for your successful foray down pathways to understanding.

CHAPTER 1

LEARNING-FOCUSED CLASSROOMS:
Patterns of Practice

Your new word processing software arrives. You load it onto your computer and are about to use it for the first time. A disconcerting new format and an array of unfamiliar icons appear before you. As you struggle to make sense of this new program, you draw on your experiences with technology, as well as your strategies for learning. As you experiment with the program, refer to the manual and experiment some more, you become increasingly comfortable with the program basics.

Each learner and each learning experience is unique; yet we can identify patterns and make generalizations about the learning process. Designing effective learning environments requires a clear understanding of and attention to both commonalities and differences in the learners and the learning.

Learning About Learning

Since ancient times, how humans learn has been a subject for philosophers, poets and scientists. This curiosity continues to drive much exploration by current researchers and thoughtful classroom teachers. The picture that is emerging from studies in cognitive psychology, strategic instruction and teaching for transfer offers a redefinition of learning that has clear implications for today's classroom practice. The most significant change is the shift in the orientation of instruction from teaching-centered to learning-focused. This shift centers instruction on the learner and learning processes and away from the teacher and teaching processes. This is not an easy shift. Like the learning process itself, this shift can be uncomfortable and fraught with uncertainty. The comfort of presenting the content and covering the material must be released to embrace the learners' interactions with concepts, skills and ideas. With this orientation, we come to realize that there is and probably never was one lesson being taught or one lesson being learned. There are as many lessons as learners and as many useful new questions as answers.

EFFECTIVE LEARNERS:
Link new information to prior knowledge
Engage with process and content simultaneously
Access and organize information
Require internal and external mediation
Need others to articulate and elaborate meaning
Employ cognitive and metacognitive strategies
Resolve disequilibrium through inquiry and experimentation
Search for and pursue personal learning goals

Table 1

Each of the practitioners described in the introduction to this book has woven this knowledge into the design of their learning environments. The central elements of effective practice illustrated by these vignettes are organized by thoughtful application of powerful patterns and practices in learning-focused classrooms.

The acronym in Table 1 organizes these patterns into a holistic description of effective learning. Together, these eight attributes offer important information for organizing productive learning environments.

Eight Learning Patterns

1. Effective learners link new information to prior knowledge.

Meaningful learning is an interactive and cumulative process which continually connects a learner with new information. Skilled learners are observant, strategic and thoughtful in linking new information to prior knowledge. Access to prior knowledge is a key ingredient of learning success. Background knowledge creates a context and foundation for new material. Unsuccessful students often do not have the skills for linking previous learnings to new information. They often lack essential retrieval strategies. Prior knowledge and experience remains inaccessible for these students.

The instructional challenge is to help students get in touch with what they already know, either through recall of previously learned material or by making context setting connections to daily life and personal histories. Visualizing the neighborhood around the school, complete with sounds, textures and aromas creates a template for examining other neighborhoods in other settings, either real or imagined. Describing the behavior of raindrops as they strike the hood of a freshly waxed car sets the scene for an exploration of the principles of adhesion and cohesion in a physical science lesson.

Learners need a repertoire of strategies to help them access this knowledge, as well as strategies for organizing new information into patterns which will help them make connections and integrate new understandings.

2. Effective learners engage with process and content simultaneously.

Process skills and content knowledge are not easily separated. The ways of knowing in a specific content area are as important as the discrete bits of information and organizing principles of the domain. How we come to know what we know is a vital underpinning for developing confidence as a learner. There are different ways of knowing in the various content areas. The cognitive and metacognitive skills of reading are different than the underlying skills in mathematics. The habits of inquiry in the social sciences differ from the research methods of biology and physics. Content and process intertwine, with one supporting the other. Explicit strategy instruction is as important as explicit content instruction. The trick is to anticipate which strategies support content learning and which content knowledge makes strategy learning memorable.

Motivating students' mental engagement is critical to success. Engaging instruction is student-centered, designed to instill a sense of wonderment, build self-esteem and foster creativity. Open-ended experiences, with no "right or wrong" answers allow students to practice generating alternatives, consider consequences, and choose action based on best judgment. In this way content comes alive as knowledge and skills are applied in context actively and interactively.

When students are given a choice in the when, what and how of learning, they are more likely to embrace learning goals and increase their commitment to learning tasks. This idea is particularly important for students who feel they have little control over many aspects of their lives. Teachers who provide flexibility will most often get a higher level of responsibility from their students. You can offer choice in assignment time frames, level of difficulty, type of final product, method for task completion, reading or research materials, and peers with whom to work.

3. Effective learners access and organize information.

The ability to organize information is fundamental to effective thinking and learning. Skilled learners are able to organize information by recognizing and developing organizing patterns both "inside and outside" one's head. Successful learners are able to sort the information that exists in their heads and categorize or classify new information that is connected, or they create a new schema or category, either temporarily or permanently, to integrate this new information. Story sequence and story patterns are examples of information organizing strategies from the primary classroom. Sorting and classifying extends through much of mathematics and science. Comparing and contrasting cuts across all content areas.

Transferring organizing schemes and strategies from one area to another is often challenging. Strategies, like much content knowledge, are often context bound. Confident learners can articulate a menu of strategies and use their organizational abilities to frame loosely structured information; to sort and select what is important from what is not; to sequence information as it is processed or applied; to integrate and synthesize new knowledge and to reframe prior knowledge.

Learning-focused teachers move from isolated skills lessons to learning strategies lessons, sending the message to students that information gains value when we understand it and apply it. In this way, students gain a tool kit for tinkering with, shaping and connecting information. Visual organizers are prime examples from this tool kit. Venn diagrams, story maps and concept maps graphically display patterns and connections. These and other visual organizers such as sequence charts, classification trees and attribute webs provide a common language for thinking. Teaching students these tools, along with consistently modeling them, provides cues for thinking, frameworks for accessing and retaining information and transfer of learning to other settings. These tools then become a lifetime gift of education.

4. Effective learners require internal and external mediation.

In the learning-focused classroom, students and teachers are partners in inquiry. They are reflective, pondering possibilities and applying insights from previous experiences. Learning occurs best when these practices are intentional, systematic and explicit.

Mediate in its Latin origins means "in the middle." In the learning-focused classroom, concepts, facts, opinions and strategies occupy the midspace between teacher and learners and between individual learners and other learners. Such teachers focus their students' attention on critical aspects of the subject at hand and offer ways to think about and explore new material. Tools for thinking are modeled and practiced, as are ways of thinking about one's thinking. These intellectual resources are the prime focus of mediation. For example, developing and strategically applying problem-solving skills becomes the focus of the math lesson, along with when and how to apply appropriate computational skills. When reading in the content areas, students describe their information-organizing strategies. They learn to articulate what they know and what they are still puzzled by and they identify questions to guide further reading.

In a mediative environment, open-ended questions are the norm and both praise and criticism are limited. Students are encouraged to articulate "thinking-in-progress" as they experiment with ideas and materials. The goal here is to transfer the external mediative voice of the teacher to the inner voice of the student as he or she learns the ways of knowing in the various content areas. This self-talk and student-to-student talk guides the work on topics at hand and provides ways of focusing on and thinking about materials and ideas.

Mediative teachers and their learners mutually develop challenging goals and criteria for success for units and projects. Reflection and self-assessment along the way are critical components of such classrooms. In these settings, student journals and learning logs are valuable resources for tracking both learning and learning processes.

5. Effective learners need others to articulate and elaborate meaning.

Learners construct meaning, both personally and socially. Joining with other learners in shared problem solving, public discussion and thinking aloud increases individual learner's capacities, adds to the collective knowledge of the class and demonstrates the importance of shared information processing and shared skills refinement.

When students recognize the need for problem-solving strategies and have the opportunity to interact with others to generate, discuss, and practice, their thinking and problem-solving skills improve. Group work, concept development activities and visual structures for organizing information such as graphic organizers and story maps collectively engage students with details, relationships and shared meaning-making. Case studies, problem scenarios and simulations, structured for group interaction give students a safe environment in which to take risks, to better prepare them for less supportive, more treacherous lessons in life.

Assignments which require students to apply new learnings, particularly in novel situations, integrate understandings and increase the likelihood of transfer. These activities move students towards both independence as learners and interdependence as members of a learning community.

6. Effective learners employ cognitive and metacognitive strategies.

Successful learners actively adopt a problem-solving approach and actively expand their repertoires of cognitive and metacognitive strategies. For example, effective readers recognize when they have lost meaning during reading and have multiple methods for checking their understanding. They purposely apply reading strategies and know when and how to apply word analysis and comprehension skills to actively make meaning from text.

Having and knowing that one has a selection of strategies to draw upon are hallmarks of confident learners. Their teachers carefully draw out the underlying thinking required by the content and processes of the topic and of individual lessons. Explicit teaching of thinking joins content learning to form the connection between minds and facts. The science lesson is infused with the processes of observing, describing, and recording along with direct instruction in ways of framing questions in a science-like way, shaping hypotheses and drawing and defending conclusions based on data and supportable inferences. When coupled with meaningful content, the cognitive skills of a particular content domain come to life and minds develop.

7. Effective learners resolve disequilibrium through inquiry and experimentation.

Disequilibrium and the uncertainty of not knowing are milestones on the pathway of any new learning. Knowing what one does not know is as important a learning resource as knowing what one does know. The challenge both emotionally and cognitively is to give up or set aside a comfortable theory or idea in pursuit of deeper understanding.

Disequilibrium occurs when new data or impressions can no longer be fit into existing ways of thinking. Less confident learners are tempted to discard or distort information to preserve existing mental models. For example, in the learning of mathematics problem solving, many students cling to the notion that whatever the problem says, it is best to subtract the smaller number from any larger number. This "rule-of-thumb" works for a time but causes difficulties with more complex problems, especially those with negative numbers.

The skills of inquiry and experimentation with materials, ideas and concepts become essential habits of mind for a lifetime. Learning-focused teachers support learners through this not-knowing phase by focusing on process skills development, theory building, theory testing and content-specific research and problem-solving skills. They provide a learning environment where it is safe to experiment and trial and error are valued. They also honor disequilibrium by taking a coaching stance with learners to help them clarify where they are in their thinking and where they might go next to resolve their own questions.

8. Effective learners search for and pursue personal learning goals.

Learning is not simply the result of experience. Learning results from the processing of experience and is supported and accelerated by skillful mediation. Such mediation helps learners make meaning and forges connection with prior learning and personal goals.

Deep intellectual engagement occurs when tasks are relevant to the learners' current interests or needs. To see oneself as a maker of meaning and as a member of a meaning-making community elevates learning tasks and places the learning of skills and facts in a richer context. Personal and collective goals are essential to this work.

Learning is a goal-driven activity. When learners feel like they own these goals, motivation and enthusiasm increase. The seeds for later success are sown in the way tasks are organized and presented to students.

To develop an identity as a learner is to see oneself as an active participant in the learning process. The pursuit of goal setting and goal achievement is taught through modeling, mediating and reflecting on both the learning in process and on the processes of learning.

Throughout the remainder of this book you will encounter maps and guideposts for pursuing pathways to understanding. You will find practical ideas, specific activities and effective strategies to ensure a successful journey. The adventure will be both challenging and rewarding, whether you follow in the footsteps of others or blaze your own new trails.

The adventure will be both challenging and rewarding, whether you follow in the footsteps of others or blaze your own new trails.

CHAPTER 2

PATTERNS & PRACTICES:
A Teaching/Learning Cycle

As you peek into the classroom, the entire class has their eyes closed. The teacher verbally guides the students up and down the aisles of a large supermarket. She vividly describes the sounds, scents and colors of the various departments. As students are visualizing the products and displays, she asks them to imagine all the places that they might find numbers. Once the teacher finishes the visualization process, the students form trios to generate specific examples of numbers in action. Each team brainstorms examples of specific products and the weights, measurements and pricing structures related to them. These then become the springboard for a lesson on unit pricing.

Activating prior knowledge and linking it to the learning at hand is a fundamental practice in teaching for connection-making. Further learning in this unit will build upon these real world connections. These connections facilitate the application of knowledge and skills in and outside of school.

The Pathways Learning Model

Learning is a continual, developmental process in which individuals move through a series of phases. During this process the ways in which the learner relates to the information evolves. Think of learning something new as embarking on a long journey to an unknown territory. Initially, we acquire concrete information and the rote learning of relatively isolated facts. The terrain is strange, but we have some referents from previous experiences. Gradually we find ourselves primarily memorizing landmarks, and the names of important places. As we progress, we begin to discern patterns and relationships between discrete pieces of information, organizing it into an overview of the new territory. A schema or integrated map develops. We then have a global understanding, concepts which can be interpreted and applied to deepen understandings. At this stage alternative routes to navigate from one place to another begin to appear, and we can transfer understandings to new settings.

As we engage in new learning, we travel through three phases which correspond to the input, process, and output nature of learning tasks. Various models of thinking use different language to describe these phases of learning. All agree that different skills and strategies are employed by strategic learners at each phase. In the first phase we prepare for learning. In the second phase we explore and process information. In the third phase we apply, organize and integrate new information.

The learning-focused teacher organizes instruction in phases and is mindful of the developmental, nonlinear nature of learning. At each phase it is important to encourage students to pause, check, process, continue with or redirect their thinking. Our current knowledge about learning informs us that we must support students in making connections; connections between what they know and what they are learning, between what they are learning and the opportunity for application in a variety of contexts; and between the relevance of their newly gained understandings and their own lives.

The teaching/learning cycle presented here is the foundation of The Pathways Learning Model, which offers a framework for instructional design which applies current research to teaching for connectedness. This framework organizes instruction for connecting new information to existing understanding, discovering relationships, and integrating concepts for application and transfer. It creates a unity of knowledge which is functional, relevant and available for further learning.

The teaching/learning cycle defines three phases of instruction: 1) activating and engaging; 2) exploring and discovering and 3) organizing and integrating. These phases occur within a learning environment where teachers manage, mediate, model, and monitor; providing purposeful tasks, ongoing authentic assessment and structured group work. Focus on thoughtful processing, specific thinking skills and hands-on application is a key component of each phase.

Phase One:
Activating and Engaging

Meaningful learning is an interactive and cumulative process which occurs between a learner and new information. Effective learners are active, strategic, thoughtful and constructive in linking new information to prior knowledge. There is a strong connection between success in integrating new information and the level of background knowledge that the student brings to the situation. Ensuring that students access and bring their background knowledge to a learning task is crucial to their success.

Students who have been unsuccessful in a learning situation often do not have strategies for linking previous learnings to new information. For these students, prior knowledge is unavailable. Strategies to provide access to what learners already know, as well as strategies for organizing new information into patterns which will help them make connections and integrate new understandings are necessary for successful learning.

The *activating and engaging* phase is a launch point for learning. When organizing opportunities for activating and engaging, learning-focused teachers are aware of three critical functions. Activating and engaging activites enable students to 1) engage prior knowledge and understandings, 2) expand the mutual knowledge base by using individual and group work to organize an exchange of information, and 3) surface and articulate frames of reference that students are bringing to the learning situation. This phase also provides an opportunity for mental rehearsal, encouraging and supporting participation from all learners.

For those students who do not have success in recognizing or accessing what they bring to a learning task, the activating and engaging phase provides strategies for making prior experience available.

Generally, activating and engaging calls for generative and associative thinking. Activities like brainstorming, identifying, listing, and envisioning are particularly powerful. In addition, during this phase, the strategic learner will be setting the purpose for the task, considering and choosing specific learning or problem-solving strategies, forming predictions or questions, or looking for cues to begin organizing information.

The Pathways Learning Model

Activating and Engaging

Engage prior knowledge, skills, and understandings

Expand the knowledge base for individuals and groups

Surface and articulate frames of reference

Organizing and Integrating

Synthesize and represent information

Develop frameworks and models

Catalog and index new understandings

Managing
Modeling
Mediating
Monitoring

Exploring and Discovering

Examine and differentiate information in light of current schema

Investigate hypotheses, concepts, and principles

Reconsider and tentatively refine schema

Organizing Principles of Learning-focused Classrooms

Each phase of the Pathways Learning Model is purposefully designed to support current learning theory. The framework is implemented in a learning environment where student engagement with information and materials (authentic tasks) and with fellow students (interactive group work) combines with conscious monitoring of student success and instructional effectiveness (on-going assessment).

Phase Two:
Exploring and Discovering

During the *exploring and discovering* phase, students process and sort as they engage with the new material and with each other. Learners connect new information to prior knowledge activated in the preparation phase. Thinking focuses on analysis, inference making, explaining and determining cause-effect relationships.

Learners compare and contrast information, identify gaps, consider new ideas and raise new questions. They monitor understanding by metacognitive self-questioning, such as "does this make sense; what do I know now, what do I need to know?"

The Pathways Learning Model

Organizing and Integrating

- classifying
- defining
- dev. analogies
- dev. metaphors
- evaluating
- generalizing
- interpreting
- prioritizing
- reflecting
- representing
- sequencing
- seriating
- sorting
- summarizing
- symbolizing
- synthesizing

Declarative

Procedural

Conditional

Activating and Engaging

- associating
- brainstorming
- enumerating
- estimating
- forecasting
- hypothesizing
- identifying
- predicting
- problem posing
- recalling
- speculating
- visualizing

Exploring and Discovering

- analyzing
- comparing
- computing
- contrasting
- describing
- distinquishing
- experimenting
- explaining
- identifying
- inferring
- measuring
- observing
- questionin
- relating
- seeking causality
- seeking effects

Cognitive Processes in Learning-Focused Classrooms

Strategies in each phase of the Pathways Learning Model cue specific types of student thinking. The Activating and Engaging phase prompts generative and associative thinking; Exploring and Discovering exercises processing skills; and the Organizing and Integrating phase directs the learner towards synthesis and evaluation. The graphic above displays the recursive nature of learning. Although the instructional design identifies strategies in each phase of the Model, an engaged learner's thinking will move within and among each phase in a variety of ways while moving towards deeper understanding.

Learning-focused teachers support student discovery by organizing students into groups which are actively and directly involved in learning activities which are nonroutine and ill-structured. This encourages experimentation and problem solving. They can structure the opportunity for students to manipulate materials, explore a range of perspectives, and grapple with complex issues. The problems are open-ended and can have many possible correct responses. Success includes methods to demonstrate the problem-solving process as well as the solution.

Hands-on activities, problem-based learning, and case studies allow students to explore and discover together. Thus, the learning-focused teacher emphasizes the notion that we are all smarter together than any one of us is alone.

Phase Three:
Organizing and Integrating

During the *organizing and integrating* phase students begin to "own what is now known." At this stage effective learners integrate their recent experiences and make connections between the new information and what they already know. They expand and refine their existing thinking patterns, or create new ones to incorporate their evolving understandings. Previously held concepts may be confirmed, refined or abandoned. To help them make sense of and retain new learnings they identify relevant examples and make personal applications.

Activities during this phase include summarizing, categorizing, mapping or graphic outlining, confirming or revising hypotheses and predictions, and generating examples and non-examples to test out new theories. Extending and elaborating new ideas also occurs when learners make novel applications or generate examples which require transfer

to different situations. By mediating students' connection making, teachers create a bridge over which learning transfers to other contexts.

Learning-Focused Environments: The Teacher as Master Weaver

Learning-focused teachers integrate the threads of effective practice, weaving the patterns and themes that are the fabric of dynamic learning environments. They manage resources for high engagement and high success. They organize instruction and scaffold learning tasks to ensure high achievement for all learners. Learning-focused teachers model a commitment to continuous learning and mediate the students' own meaning-making process. They monitor continually, and with a variety of methods, to determine the appropriateness of their curricular objectives, the effectiveness of their instructional design and the levels of successful learning for all students.

Managing

Learning-focused teachers manage the resources of the learning environment to organize authentic, meaningful instructional activities, and provide group experiences which support student learning. The classroom described in Chapter One featured carefully structured time, physical space, instructional materials and lesson formats. The interaction patterns enabled students to organize information, develop conceptual understanding, recognize patterns and themes, and learn from their own endeavors. Academic tasks were structured with clear directions, clear objectives and clear procedures. The teachers provided time and space for social information processing with peers. They managed curricular decisions, moving from isolated skills lessons to learning strategy lessons, sending the message to students that acquiring information is most useful when we understand it and can apply it.

Scaffolding

The scaffold is one of the most powerful managing strategies in the learning-focused teacher's repertoire. Just as the construction metaphor might suggest, an instructional scaffold is designed to be a temporary structure which is made available on an as-needed basis and removed when it is no longer necessary. Scaffolds allow learners to reach higher than they might without this support. Assistance may include verbal or visual prompts, gestural cues, remodeling of a strategy, structural formats, additional examples or whatever is necessary to ensure students' success in a learning task that might otherwise have been beyond them. Scaffolding strategy instruction gives students the confidence to strive for independent success, knowing that assistance will be available if necessary.

Scaffolds can be created for both process and product. For example, a classroom chart which posts the procedures or rules for brainstorming (see FLOW on p. 25), or examples of a particular social skill the class is working on are visual cues which remind students of important process norms. A simple paragraph frame (see p. 37) is a powerful example of a product scaffold.

Scaffolds need to be both intentionally constructed and just as intentionally decomposed. Once students become increasingly independent, and have integrated the thinking and skills required for success, it is important to remember to remove the support.

These simple structures and purposeful teaching behaviors build capacity; creating a classroom where more learners are more successful more of the time—particularly at increasingly complex tasks.

Modeling

Ralph Waldo Emerson is credited as saying, "What you do speaks so loudly, they can't hear what you say." We agree; the power of modeling cannot be underestimated. Learning-focused teachers model metacognition; they think out loud about their own approach to a

Scaffolds can be created for both process and product. For example, a classroom chart which posts the procedures or rules for brainstorming (see FLOW on p. 25)

Instructional Scaffolds

- Develop independent and strategic learners

- Support high performance learning levels early on

- Foster confidence and success

Designer's Mind: Developing Scaffolds

1. Project potential problem areas.
   In this (unit, topic, lesson, etc.) where might my students get stuck?

2. Analyze the task/process/content.
   How might I break this task/process into increments?
   What are the "walk-away" ideas?

3. Identify strategies necessary for success.
   How do effective learners achieve success with this task/process?

4. Identify prerequisite learnings.
   What fundamental concepts, facts, knowledge, skills, attitudes are prerequisites to this learning?

5. Design prototypes.
   What models of process or products would support learning success?

6. Determine learner's focus.
   Where and how does the learner's attention need to be focused along the way?

problem or learning task. They describe their own processes for creating an effective plan, or reflecting on a learning experience. They model application of specific strategies and what to do when stuck or unsure, as well as a willingness to learn through trial and error.

They demonstrate the conventions of written, oral and mathematical language, through usage and displays; and exhibit the rigor of precision and high standards for learning.

Further, they display critical dispositions, such as curiousity, flexibility and perserverance. Most importantly, they model their commitment to learning by sharing their own learning challenges and goals, and by learning with and from their students on a daily basis.

Mediating

Learning-focused teachers mediate the interaction between the student and the learning environment; anticipating confusion, providing support, facilitating the acquisition of information, providing feedback and coaching students towards independence as learners.

We borrow the term mediating from the work of Reuven Feuerstein, an Israeli psychologist who developed the concept of cognitive mediation. Cognitive mediation is a three-point interaction between the teacher (as mediator), the learner (an individual student or group of

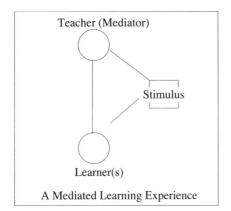

Teacher (Mediator)

Stimulus

Learner(s)

A Mediated Learning Experience

students), and a stimulus. The stimuli can include a body of information (text, video, music, etc.) a demonstration or the observation of some natural phenomena, or any event. Mediation can occur prior to, during and/or following any experience.

Cognitive mediation enhances learning and increases the likelihood of transfer by deepening the meaning-making process and by developing generalizations beyond the specific event or interaction. Learning-focused teachers intentionally guide experiences to clarify their purpose and importance, and to create opportunities for students to construct understanding.

Art Costa and Robert Marzano have identified seven ways that teachers can begin to mediate the learning of their students by teaching the language of thinking. Their seven starting points suggest that teachers can:

1. Label thought processes, their own and their students', by using precise vocabulary for thinking processes.

2. Incorporate classroom questions that will require students to examine their own behavior.

3. Provide information to help students solve problems, rather than providing the solutions.

4. Give directions which require students to analyze the task and consider what resources or information they will need to perform the task successfully.

5. Be clear in defining terms, actions and descriptions by avoiding vague generalities.

6. Encourage metacognition by asking students to describe their thinking, to verbalize the questions they are asking themselves, and to plan out loud. Further, teachers can model these behaviors for their students on a regular basis.

Swingers
A Sample Lesson Using the Teaching/ Learning Cycle

This lesson illustrates the complete teaching/learning cycle. Note the three lesson phases and the teacher behaviors of managing, modeling, mediating and monitoring. Notice also the interaction between the teacher behaviors. These areas for decision making and action are not necessarily sequential. Further, they are interactive and influence each other. One example is the interplay between mediating and monitoring towards the end of this lesson.

In this lesson using swingers, students explore variables that may effect the behavior of pendulums. They will discover that the length of the pendulum is the critical variable that determines the number of swings the pendulum will make in a given unit of time. Students then create data charts and graphs to predict the number of swings new swingers will make. As is the case with most critical concepts, this topic is not limited to a single instructional period and would probably stretch over several. It is presented here in its basic form.

Managing:	
Student Interaction	Resources
Divide the class into teams of four.	**Materials for *each* team of four students**
Assign the following team roles:	**1** - plastic bag to hold the materials
• Lab Director (Timer)	**50** - learning links or jumbo paper clips
• Equipment Manager (Materials)	**6** - metal washers to fit links
• Lab Technician (Counter)	**1** - watch with second hand
• Research Assistant (Recorder)	

ACTIVATING AND ENGAGING

1. Using Brainstorm & Pass, teams generate a list of *"things that swing"*. The Research Assistant records the group's thinking. After three minutes, randomly select a reporter from each team to share greatest hits. You might want to collect this input on a class list on the chalkboard or a large piece of chart paper.

2. The Equipment Manager keeps the list for later use.

EXPLORING AND DISCOVERING

Managing:

The Equipment Manager picks up a plastic bag of links and washers for the group.

Modeling:

Demonstrate how to assemble a swinger with 12 links as the length and 2 washers clipped to the bottom link as the starting mass. Use a 13th link as the pivot point. Suspend your swinger from the 13th link, pull back on the washers and release. Count the number of times the swinger cycles in 15 seconds. NOTE: A complete cycle is over and back. This is counted as "1." Round to the nearest ° cycle. Use the 15-second block as a constant. (Cycle numbers will vary from 11–13 cycles for this first test when using plastic learning links.)

1. Have student teams assemble a 12 link–2 washer swinger and practice releasing it and counting the number of cycles in 15 seconds. The Lab Technician counts while the Lab Director monitors time. Be sure each team is using a 13th link as a pivot point and not just the 12 links or their count will vary from the rest of the class. The Research Assistant should record the number of counts per trial. Remember, half counts round up to the nearest whole.

2. After all the groups have had several practice swings, check in to see how many cycles they are counting in 15 seconds. All the groups should be within the same range. If a group's count varies greatly, observe their swinging and counting technique to determine the variation.

Mediating:

3. Ask students to suggest variables that might influence the number of cycles the swingers will make, with the time held constant at 15 seconds. List these on the chalkboard or on a piece of chart paper.

4. Have student teams test the suggested variables. Stop the class from time to time to have groups report on their findings. Eventually the variable of length will emerge as the key variable. When this happens, stop the class and have students construct a data chart similar to the following. The blanks are important. The empty spaces in the data chart will be used as part of the assessment system for this activity.

Number of Links	5		15		25		35	
Number of Cycles								

5. To test the variable of length, the teams construct swingers of varying numbers of links. They continue their experiments, as earlier, keeping the time (15 seconds) constant and filling in the data chart with the number of cycles per trial. They do not need to test every possible number of links. Varying by units of five allows a pattern to emerge. NOTE: Team roles are still in use.

6. When the table is complete, teams create a graph of their data.

ORGANIZING AND INTEGRATING

Monitoring:

1. Test students' understanding of the relationship between length and number of cycles by asking them to estimate the number of cycles a swinger of X number of links will swing. Vary this by asking how many links it would take to have a swinger that cycled X times in 15 seconds.

Mediating/Monitoring:

2. When students can make these predictions with some accuracy, have them formulate a rule for swingers (e.g., the shorter the swinger the more cycles it swings.)

3. Ask the Equipment Manager to retrieve the original brainstormed lists of things that swing. Teams examine their lists and sort between those items that obey the "law of swingers" as they now understand it and those that do not.

Extending for Transfer

• Use other materials such as string and yarn to construct swingers. The focusing question is, *"Do swingers made from these materials behave the same as the swingers made from links?"* Have students make predictions and then test them out.

• Go out to a playground and experiment with real swingers. Adjust the swings to create swingers that will swing varying numbers of cycles in a given period.

7. Highlight linguistic cues which indicate relationships, such as sequence, causality, compare/contrast and addition (e.g., *then, since, but, however,* and, *both*). (See Chapter 3, Mediating Student Thinking, for more detailed information).

Monitoring

Teaching and learning are an ongoing and reciprocal process. Teachers make purposeful choices during four distinct phases of this instructional process; while planning a lesson or unit of instruction, during the implementation of this plan; after teaching, while reflecting on the effectiveness of the instruction and then again while applying new learnings to the ongoing planning process.

Learning-focused teachers are reflective practitioners who engage in a continual cycle of self-assessment and self-directed learning based on their experiences. At each phase of decision making, these teachers monitor for the best match between instructional decisions and student success. Purposeful attention to the relationship between their own behaviors and the students' performance allows learning-focused teachers to make adjustments, modifications and refinements—in their "seat" while planning and reflecting, and on their feet while teaching.

Determinations are made about a variety of variables using multiple methods. These include the appropriateness of curricular outcomes, the effectiveness of teacher choices and behaviors on student performance, and the level of student achievement— academically and socially.

Gathering quantitative information, such as test scores, frequency of student responses, and attendance records, as well as qualitative information, such as

students' expressions of understanding or confusion, social interaction patterns, and teachers' anecdotal records, drives the continual learning about, and improvement of, practice.

Three Levels of Knowledge

Current theories in learning and knowledge acquisition make distinctions between three levels of knowledge; declarative, procedural and conditional. Declarative knowledge is knowing *what*. Facts, figures, dates and the famous people connected to historical events are all examples of declarative knowledge. Procedural knowledge is knowing *how* to do something. Examples of procedural knowledge include following directions, applying a principle or theorem, exercising a skill, such as measurement, or creating a visual display of data, such as a chart or graph. Conditional knowledge is knowing *when* or *why* to choose one strategy or process over another. Application of conditional knowledge presupposes a repertoire of learning strategies, as well as some criteria for choice-making.

Effective problem solving and decision making is contingent upon the application of conditional knowledge. While traditional classrooms engage students in sophisticated problem solving, the problems tend to be routine and highly structured. There is a correct response. In the learning-focused classroom, problems are nonroutine and ill-structured; there can be many possible appropriate responses. These problems are more "lifelike" in that the world is full of messy problems with no set answer. Conditional knowledge is applied to resolve uncertainty by making a well-thought-out choice. In fact, the process of problem-solving is as important as the final answer.

> **3 Levels of Knowledge**
>
> • **DECLARATIVE** knowing *what*
>
> • **PROCEDURAL** knowing *how*
>
> • **CONDITIONAL** knowing *when* and *why*

Pathways to Understanding: Ensuring Success for all Learners

The goal of education is success for all students. Learning-focused teaching is a way to achieve that goal by providing educators with clear methods for improving the thinking and communication skills of all students within and across content areas.

The Pathways Learning Model is designed to ensure that learning experiences will be orchestrated and structured for high engagement and increased success for all students. It will support you in creating a learning environment that integrates practical methods that connect new information with prior knowledge, create new relationships and develop conceptual understandings, and organize understandings for application and transfer.

The Model is not intended to be an exhaustive list of all possibilities. Rather, it is a template for instructional design. It provides a planning guide from which you can identify cognitive outcomes, plan relevant, content-based objectives and organize teaching for connectedness.

The strategies you will find throughout this book work within this design template to provide access to success for underachievers as well as highly motivated learners. Practical and flexible, they are designed to support your initial and continued travel on your own pathways to understanding.

The strategies you will find throughout this book work within this design template to provide access to success for underachievers as well as highly motivated learners.

Strategies
for Active
Learning

Four Box Synectics

Synectics *promotes fluid and creative thinking by "making what is familiar strange," or comparing two things that would not ordinarily be compared.* **Synectics,** *a term coined by industrial psychologists William Gordon and George Prince, was originally used as a problem-solving strategy. The term is formed from two Greek roots:* syn, *bringing together, and* ectics, *diverse elements.*

Prepare a chart or overhead transparency like the one below, covering the bottom section so that the group does not see the sentence for completion.

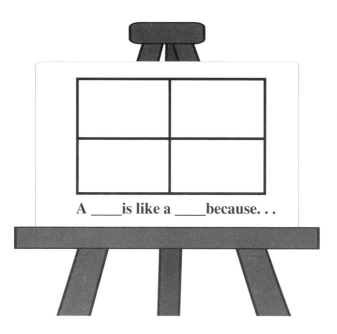

A _____ is like a _____ because. . .

Variations:
• *Any topic, concept, issue* is like *any category* because . . . .
Ex.: <u>Learning science</u> is like <u>what sport or recreational activity</u> because. . . .

• *Any topic, concept, issue* is like *a specific item* because . . . .
Ex.: <u>A productive team</u> is like <u>a forest</u> because. . . .

• Choose between two possibilities:
Ex.: <u>Photosynthesis</u> is more like ice cream or more like spaghetti because. . . .

1. Structure student groups of 3 or 4. Teams will need to identify a recorder.

2. Next, ask for four items in an assigned category (e.g., *commonly found household objects, animals, things found in a forest, recreational activities, foods*). Place one item in each of the four boxes (be sure to take whatever the group members give you—any items will work).

3. Reveal the sentence and allow groups three minutes to brainstorm completions—using each of the four items *at least once*—but going for as many completions as they can. (Reviewing rules for brainstorming is useful here; see p. 25.)

4. After three minutes, STOP. The next step is for each group to choose the two they like the best to share with the full class. Give them a minute or two, then share by table group.

SYNECTICS
makes a great prewriting activity

 See Page 102

Visual Synectics

Visual Synectics *is similar to* Synectics *but offers a visual prompt for students' brainstorming. The concrete image is a good scaffold for younger students or newly formed groups.*

1. Prepare a set of picture cards—photographs of everyday objects cut from magazines and catalogs glued to 4 x 6 index cards. A mix of organic and human-made objects seems to work best. Laminating the cards makes them more durable and longer lasting.

2. Structure student groups of 3 or 4. Randomly distribute cards to each group or let them pick one from a pile placed face down.

3. Have small groups generate responses to the following:

   • List parts, materials, functions, properties, and processes
     associated with the objects pictured on your card

4. Small groups then compare their lists to the topic or concept selected by you for comparison.

   How is _____ like <u>your picture card</u> ?

Sort Cards or Pictures

Sort cards *or* **sort pictures** *work well with any content where clear relationships exist between concepts or terms. These relationships can be part to whole, whole to part, cause and effect or any other arrangement that shows connections between the individual items.*

Directions:

Create sets of cards containing concepts, terms or pictures which will be encountered in an upcoming unit of study or reading assignment.

1. Structure students into groups of 3 or 4.
2. Distribute a card set to each group.
3. Teams sort the cards into categories or groups based on the relationships which they perceive exist between terms. After the cards are sorted, student teams create labels for their groupings.

Examples:

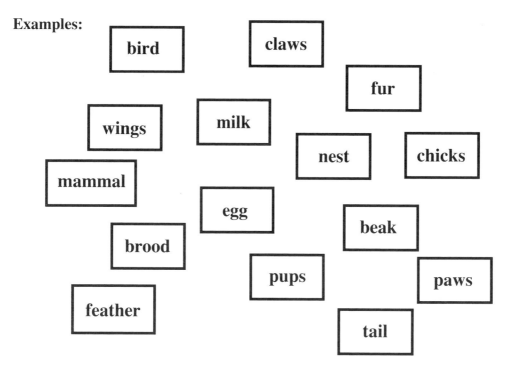

Variations:

- Give the class a topic of study.
  Have the students create the items they associate with the topic on index cards or Post-it® notes (one item per card).
  Then, in small groups, share their items and categorize, as above.
- Use picture cards with prereaders, ESL students or when teaching highly abstract concepts.

Helpful Hints: Save time in class; have students create sort cards as a homework assignment.

Brainstorm & Pass

Brainstorming has a long history as a tool for generating ideas. The term brainstorming was invented by advertising executive, Alex Osborn, in the late 1940s. **Brainstorm & Pass** *is a highly effective strategy that enhances the fundamental brainstorming process by ensuring full participation of all group members during a brainstorming session.*

Brainstorm & Pass reinforces three important messages:
1) Everyone is responsible for participating.
2) Everyone has something to contribute.
3) Time to think is valued and provided.

Directions:

1. Establish small groups and set ground rules for brainstorming. We offer the acronym FLOW as a scaffold for setting brainstorming norms:

   Flexibility and fluidity of thinking is encouraged.

   Lots of ideas is the goal; all ideas are recorded.

   Open acceptance of all ideas is necessary.

   Withhold all judgment (both criticism and praise).

2. Choose a recorder and be sure that each student has something to write on and something to write with.

3. Explain to the groups that they will offer ideas on the topic *in turn,* starting to the right of the recorder. The group must wait for each student to either a) offer an idea, or b) say "Pass." Passing means "I can't think of anything right now." Students who pass still get their turn during the next go around.
   Remember: The recorder is included and has a turn in the process.

4. After approximately 3 minutes, call STOP.

Brainstorm & Pass is a powerful way to increase participation and prevent students who are most vocal, most knowledgeable or most passionate about a topic from dominating a session.

Helpful Hints: Set a minimum target for the number of ideas to be generated. Time pressure helps keep groups focused. Keep time short.

See Page 103

Brainstorm and Categorize

Brainstorming is a powerful method for surfacing prior knowledge and engaging learners in associative and generative thinking. Once ideas are generated, the interactive process can be extended in a variety of ways. **Brainstorm and Categorize** *is one such extension that supports continued exploration and discovery.*

Directions:

1. Structure groups for brainstorming (see previous page).

2. After ideas on a topic have been brainstormed, students group the items in categories sharing like attributes. Titles are then generated for each group. One option is to have students record their ideas on Post-it® notes, which can then be grouped and rearranged as categories emerge.

Energy

History	Measurement	Alternative Sources
Muscles	Calories	Passive Solar
Fire	Watts	Geothermal
Wind	BTUs	Hydroelectric
Water	Joule	Biomass
Sun	Temperature	Photovoltaic

3. Record ideas and categories and post on large charts. Add items as the unit progresses.

   The idea-generation process surfaces untapped knowledge and enriches the collective knowledge base. The charts offer a picture of the current working knowledge of the students. Posting the charts keeps the information available for continued thinking and extensions.

Modality Brainstorming

Modality Brainstorming *taps learning style differences that appear to be hardwired into the brain. The brain stores and processes information in four primary modalities: visual, kinesthetic, auditory and olfactory/gustatory.*

To test this theory have students brainstorm for several minutes on a selected topic. Example: How do you know it is September in (your part of the country) ?

Give students 3–4 minutes to generate a respectable list, then stop them and have the recorder apply the following procedure.

Directions to Students:

1. Examine your list and draw a line after the 10th item.

2. Read each item and ask the person in your group who generated the idea how that idea occurred in his or her brain. Was it a picture, a feeling, a sound, or a taste or smell?

3. Label each of the 10 ideas using the following code.

V	**Visual—pictures and images**
K	**Kinesthetic—feelings both physical and emotional**
A	**Auditory—sounds**
O/G	**Olfactory/Gustatory—smells and tastes**

It is important that the person who generated the idea be the one who labels the modality. All people do not process information the same way.

Note: Some ideas may require double coding because the idea is stored in two modalities. For example, an image of a fire may be a picture (V) and a feeling (K). This would be coded VK.

4. Count up the number of modalities used to generate the list. By using just 10 items it is possible to establish percentages of modality dominance for the class. (The population as a whole is roughly divided into 40% visual, 40% kinesthetic and 20% auditory.)

5. You can now stretch the brainstorming by having students use their nondominant modalities to generate new ideas. Novel ideas are more likely to occur when we stretch beyond our normal ways of processing.

Brainstorm With Side Trips

Side trips *is an idea-generation strategy that builds on* Modality Brainstorming *to help students shift perspectives and gain fresh sources of ideas. A side trip is a teacher-guided imaginary journey through another place, thing, persona or time period. At selected stops along the way, students are encouraged to imagine the sights, sounds, smells and tastes that they encounter.*

Side trips fall into several categories:

1. **Places,** specific locations from near and far, rich in detail and information.
2. **Things and objects** that might be associated with the topic.
3. **Personas,** people and animals that offer new perspectives.
4. **Time periods,** past and future.

Specific side-trip examples are easy to come up with once a topic develops for idea generation. As students become familiar with the strategy, they can help develop areas for side trips as well as the ideas associated with the side trip.

Students can use traditional brainstorming or a brainstorm-and-pass pattern. In a study of the seasons, idea generation for each season might develop along the following lines.

Students brainstorm for approximately 2 minutes at each side trip; then stop and begin the next.

How do you know it is Spring, Summer, Fall, Winter?

Places:
- at the mall
- in your neighborhood
- in the city, in the country

Things/objects:
- by reading the Sunday paper
- by looking in the refrigerator
- by what's in your backpack

Personas:
- if you were a dog/cat/horse
- if you were blind
- if you loved sports

Time periods:
- when you were a baby
- 100 years ago (in our town)
- 100 years from now

Carousel Brainstorming

Carousel Brainstorming *is a wonderful strategy when you and the class need a shift of energy—and it's especially good for your kinesthetic learners. As the class moves from station to station, all learners recognize their value as resources to each other.*

Managing:

Post large sheets of newsprint at various points on the walls around the room. There should be one sheet for each of 4–6 students. Each sheet has a question or topic written on it relating to an area of study.

Divide students into teams of 4–6 and assign a starting point at one of the newsprint stations. Give each team a different color marking pen. The pens travel with the teams. This builds in accountability for the teams and pinpoints the source of any errors or major misconceptions.

Directions to Student Teams:

1. Stand in front of one sheet of newsprint.

2. Choose a recorder and a facilitator if needed.

3. Quickly brainstorm responses to the posted question and write your responses on the paper.

4. At the signal (after an appropriate time interval), pass the marker to another group member and move one sheet to the right.

5. Repeat the process at each new station.

6. Continue until each team has responded to all the questions.

7. Return to your original sheet and review the items there. Place a question mark by any that you question.

Variations:

*   When teams return to their original question or topic, provide fresh paper and have them categorize the responses that they and their classmates generated.

*   The topics on each chart can stay the same, but each round can add a different level of thinking or complexity to the required responses.

Helpful Hints:

Create one chart more than the number of teams so there will always be an empty station. Allow teams to self-time, moving to a new chart when they are ready.

For classrooms without available wall space, put each topic/question on a clipboard and have student teams pass the clipboards in rotation.

Chart headings can be questions, such as:
*   What does it need to live?
*   Where are you most likely to find it?
*   What are some possible causes for _____?

or

sub-topics in a unit of study, such as:
*   Regions in the U.S. (NE, SW, Midwest, SE)
*   Different habitats (forest, desert, tundra, grasslands)
*   Geometric shapes (parallelogram, rhombus, sphere)
*   Elements of literature (plot, setting, characters) or various authors

Idea, Category and Web

Idea, category and web *is another brainstorming modification. It helps students develop categorization skills and scaffolds word web creation. Brainstorming groups tend to follow chains of ideas. Each idea triggers associations and relationships. In many cases, the chains run out of links and group energy falters. This strategy anticipates these problems by continually forcing new category development.*

Directions:

1. Prepare a T-chart. Label the columns IDEA and CATEGORY.

2. Present a topic for idea and category generation. Have neighbors connect for several minutes to share ideas and possible categories.

3. Call on a student to offer an idea. Record it in the idea column.

4. Generate a category label. Have the student who offered the idea or other students propose a category within which the idea fits and record this in the appropriate column.

   Each category may be used only once. The goal is to generate broad categories to elaborate with details during the webbing phase.

5. Continue the process. Develop 6–12 idea/category pairs. This is usually enough for a rich web.

6. Draw a web diagram with the category labels in place.

7. Add details to the web, category by category.

Whales	
Idea	**Category**
Baleen	Food Gathering
Flukes	Body Parts
Whaling	Human Impact
Barnacles	Parasites

Step 1–5

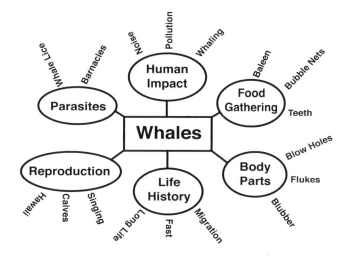

Steps 6 and 7

5 - 3 - 1

5 - 3 - 1 *is an organizing and integrating strategy that involves small groups in surfacing, comparing, sorting and synthesizing key learning and experience.*

This strategy also uses the familiar pattern of individual to small-group to full-class interaction. Apply 5 - 3 - 1 to the current topic of study, or to a recent event (such as a field trip or assembly) that the students have experienced.

Directions to Students:

1. Individually, jot down five words that come to mind when you think about _TOPIC_ (your choices may be about the content, your feelings, some things you remember, important or special vocabulary, words that describe, etc.).

2. Share your items with your table group, and choose three.

3. Now, as a group, choose one word which captures your thinking about this topic; it may be one of your three, or a different word entirely.

4. What & Why: Be ready to share your choice—the word you chose and some reasons for choosing it.

Variations:

• Skip steps 1 and 2 and ask small groups to create a One-Word Summary.

• As a scaffold, give students a list of 15–20 words. Have individual students choose five, then follow process as above.

---

5 - 3 - 1

1. On your own, write down five words:

2. Our three words are:

3. Our group's word is:

A See Page 105

Circle Map

The Circle Map is a simple yet powerful graphic organizer that helps students focus their thinking and make connections between ideas. Its purpose is to help learners put things in context to better understand their own and others' points of view. It works best with small groups of three to four students working with markers and chart paper. The chart paper recording builds in greater accountability and shared ownership among team members.

Directions:

1. On a piece of chart paper, each team draws a large circle with a smaller circle in the center. Be sure to leave the corners free for later use.

2. The small circle holds a word, symbol, or picture that represents or labels an object, person, concept or idea being studied.

3. In the outside circle students list words and phrases they associate with the idea in the inner circle. These words and phrases establish the context within which students are currently thinking about the content at hand.

4. After sufficient working time, have students step back from their maps and in the upper right-hand corners, list categories that hold the ideas they have generated thus far. One option here is to swap papers with a neighboring group and categorize the new list.

5. Now students should be ready to consciously surface their frames of reference. These are listed in the lower corners. Focusing questions:
    • What prior knowledge influences your view?
    • What are the cultural and personal influences on your perspective?
    • How do your present roles (student, athlete, musician, son, daughter) influence your point of view?

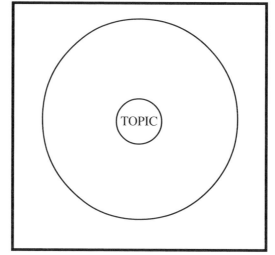

Source: Hyerle, David. (1990). *Designs for Thinking Connectively*. Cary, NC: Innovative Sciences.

Semantic Mapping

Semantic mapping *is a useful strategy for activating and engaging and for pre- and post-assessment of learning. A major strength of this strategy is that it helps students to construct a model for organizing and integrating the information that they are learning. Semantic maps can be used prior to a reading assignment or on a larger scale, as a kickoff to a new unit of study. As the unit progresses, new information can be added to the maps.*

Directions:

1. Choose a key word or topic related to a unit of study.
2. Write the word on an overhead transparency or on a sheet of chart paper.
3. Ask students to think of as many words and ideas as they can that relate to the focal word.
4. Write the words on the map in clusters or categories.
5. Have the students suggest labels for the categories and write them on the map.
6. If there are any key vocabulary words that are important to the comprehension of a reading assignment and students do not mention them, add them to the map with a red marker or pen.
7. Discussion of the semantic map is the most important part of the lesson. This helps students become aware of their current thinking and helps them to see relationships between words and ideas.
8. After the reading assignment, or as the unit progresses, new words and categories can be added to the map. Use different colors of ink to show that this information was not known prior to the reading or unit study.

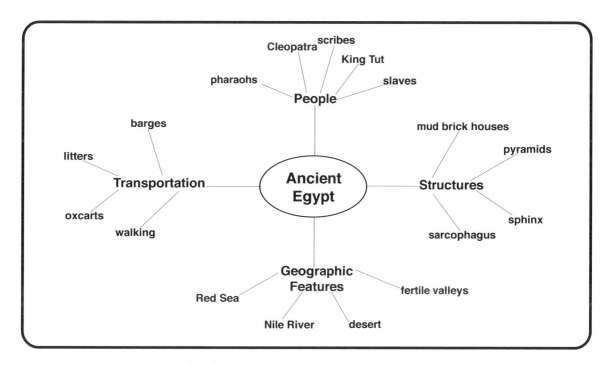

Initial Student Map for Ancient Egypt

Semantic Feature Analysis

Semantic feature analysis draws on the ways information is stored by category in memory. This strategy has a wide variety of classroom applications that help students to better understand critical vocabulary and key concepts in a reading selection or unit of study.

Students draw on their background knowledge to generate relationships between ideas and topics within a category. The key features of these words are displayed in a grid, which visually organizes and clearly presents important relationships.

Semantic feature analysis promotes vocabulary development in a wide variety of classroom situations. The technique helps students develop semantic precision by examining the pattern of pluses and minuses to sort out key features of the words they are learning.

Directions:

1. Select a category. To introduce the strategy start with categories that are concrete and familiar, such as tools, pets or fruits.

2. List words in the category. Down the left side of a large sheet of paper or on a transparency or the chalkboard, list four to five words that name objects or concepts related to the category. These words should be familiar to the students.

3. List and add features. In a row across the top of the chart, list traits and properties shared by some of the words. Ask students to supply additional traits to expand this list. The list of such features can be quite extensive.

4. Determine feature possession. Walk students through the grid, asking them to determine whether the words listed down the left side typically possesses each of the features displayed along the top. Use a plus sign (+) to indicate that the word usually possesses this feature. Use a negative sign (–) to indicate that it does not. A question mark can be entered when students do not know or are unsure. These then become placeholders and cues for focused reading and research.

5. Add more words and features. Once the basic grid is completed, have students generate additional words for the category and additional features for analysis.

6. Complete the grid. Have students complete the grid, adding pluses, minuses and question marks as needed. Encourage them to use reference materials to verify their answers.

7. Examine and discuss the grid. When the grid is completed, encourage students to examine and discuss patterns they see there. Have them note similarities and differences among the words. Support students in forming generalizations about the words in the category as well as focusing on what makes each word unique.

Features

Planets	Closer to Sun than Earth	Larger than Earth	Smaller than Earth	Has rings	Has moon(s)		
Earth							
Jupiter							
Mars							
Mercury							
Neptune							
Pluto							
Saturn							
Uranus							
Venus							

Shapes to find on the trip to the Fire Station

	△	▥	◍
Equipment			
Truck			
Station			

Source: Jane Hodgkins Lyseth School, Portland, Maine

Semantic Feature Analysis
Reading and Writing Extensions

Semantic feature analysis *can be extended to develop important connections between reading and writing in the content areas. As students think about and talk through the creation of their semantic feature analysis grids they are participating in many important prewriting tasks, including predicting, hypothesizing and synthesizing.*

The grid and the accompanying discussions motivate student writers and provide concrete starting points for compositions. A variety of writing forms, including writing frames, descriptions, and questions can be developed from the information displayed on the grids.

Directions:

1. Display a grid for the selected topic.

2. Have students complete the grid adding pluses and minuses as they tap their personal knowledge of the topic. Leave cells blank if students are unsure or do not know the appropriate response.

3. Have students read the text to confirm their answers, correct their responses and seek new information. If disagreements arise, students should read from the text to support their answers.

4. Using the completed grid, ask students to develop an accurate sentence about one item on the matrix.

5. Display a model paragraph and discuss the use of the topic sentence, three sentences supplying detail and a concluding sentence.

6. Divide students into small groups to write a detailed paragraph about some other item on the grid.

7. As skills develop, the paragraph assignment can be extended to a one-page composition.

See Page 107

Features

Fruits	Many seeds	Pit	Edible skin	Inedible skin	Grown in bunches		
Apple	+	—	+	—	—		
Pear	+	—	+	—	—		
Peach	—	+	+	—	—		
Plum	—	+	+	—	—		
Grape	+	—	+	—	+		
Orange	+	—	—	+	—		
Banana	+	—	—	+	+		

PARAGRAPH FRAME

There are many different types of fruit. Fruits have different characteristics. Some fruits, such as _____ , _____ and _____ have lots of seeds, while others, such as _____ and _____ have pits. You can eat the skin of fruits like _____ , _____ and _____ , but the skin of _____ and _____ are inedible.

Concept Maps

Concept Maps *are useful tools for helping students organize information about important topics. They go beyond semantic maps and webs by showing the relationship between linked items. They display hierarchies of information as they move from big ideas to supporting details.*

To create a concept map, students place major concept words in ovals. These words are usually nouns. The ovals are connected by stems and linking words that describe the connection between the ovals.

The most general concept or biggest idea is placed in an oval at the top of the page. The words become more specific as students move down the page. Model the process before directing students to do their own.

Concept Maps can be created before, during, and after a reading assignment or an entire unit of study. They can also be used as an alternative form of assessment.

Directions:

1. List all the concepts to be mapped.

2. Pick out the main concept. Rank the remaining concepts, listing them from most general to most specific. Cluster related ideas.

3. Arrange the concepts in a downward-flowing, branching structure. In the early stages of teaching concept mapping this can be done on file cards or Post-it® notes. The cards or notes can then be rearranged as needed.

4. Connect related concepts with stems and appropriate linking words.

5. Develop cross-linkages at important connecting points.

Before and After Diagrams

Before and After Diagrams *are student-made drawings and diagrams rendered before and after a unit of study. These diagrams provide an excellent way to assess student learning.*

The pre-instruction drawings activate student thinking and provide teachers with a quick way to assess existing knowledge and misconceptions.

The simplest application of this strategy is to provide blank paper or chart paper and have students or teams of students draw or diagram details and interactions.

Another option is to provide students with basic outlines to fill in, such as a human body outline or a map without geophysical details.

Examples:

- Draw a map of the classroom, your bedroom, your neighborhood.

- Draw a specific plant or animal.

- Draw examples of selected simple machines.

- Draw a scene that captures an historical event.

- Diagram a government structure.

When assessing knowledge in this way, encourage students to include needed details. Do not allow them to use external resources. Listen to discussions and watch for behaviors that reflect problem solving.

When comparing the pre- and post-instruction diagrams, look for the accuracy of details, relationships, and organizational structures that show evidence of growth in knowledge and concepts.

Here's What! / So What?/ Now What?

Here's What!/So What?/Now What? *is a highly versatile strategy which supports students' capacity to surface and organize prior knowledge and make projections, predictions and inferences. Some ways it can be used:*

1) When introducing a new topic to assess students' understanding and prepare them for further study

2) To study current or historical events

3) To increase reading comprehension and literal and inferential reasoning

TIP: Newspaper headlines make very good "Here's Whats."

Directions:

Have students work in pairs or small teams. The Here's What! column is filled with specific facts or information (data), the So What? column is an interpretation of the data, and the Now What? column can be a prediction, an implication or a question for further study.

Here's What!	So What?	Now What?
Charlotte spins a web in Wilbur's pen.	The spider and the pig become neighbors and friends.	They will have adventures together and change each other's lives.
Charlotte spins a special web to save Wilbur's life.	Wilbur wins a blue ribbon at the fair	Wilbur is more valuable alive than dead

Here's What!	So What?	Now What?
International Space Station Moving Towards Completion		

See Page 106

Possible Sentences

Possible Sentences (Moore & Moore, 1986) *is a combination vocabulary/prediction activity designed to acquaint students with new vocabulary in their reading, guide them in verifying the accuracy of the statements they generate, and arouse curiosity about the passage to be read. Possible Sentences is best used when unfamiliar vocabulary is mixed with familiar terminology.*

Directions:

1. **Structure.** Create student groups of 3–4.

2. **List key vocabulary.** Place word list on chalkboard, overhead or on a hand-out.

3. **Elicit sentences.** Students select at least two words from the list and formulate a sentence using the words.

4. **Read the passage.** Students read individually or assign a reader to verify their sentences.

5. **Evaluate sentences for accuracy.** Where necessary, teams refine and correct their work.

6. **Generate new sentences.** Students create new sentences using additional vocabulary words and record all final accurate sentences in their notebooks.

Warts

dermatologist	electrocautery
autosuggestive cures	verrucae
polyoma virus	Pliny the Elder
nostrums	verrucose
caustic painting	spunk water
freezing	Mark Twain

Word Splash—Picture Splash

Word Splash *was originally developed as a prereading strategy by reading researcher Dorsey Hammond of Oakland University, Rochester, Michigan, who calls it the Key Word technique.*

A Word Splash is a collection of key terms or concepts selected from a chapter in a textbook, a lecture, a demonstration, or from audiovisual materials which students are about to read, see or hear. The selected terms are splashed at angles on a chart or overhead transparency. Students are asked to generate complete statements—not just words or phrases—of their predictions regarding the relationship of the term(s) to the topic. Students usually work in small groups to generate statements.

Once the statements are generated, the printed material is presented to the students. They read it together and pause after each paragraph or two to check their predictions against the data that is presented. Students should modify their statements as needed and place a question mark next to any statements which are not verified or negated. You may want to assign the roles of recorder, reader, and checker to students.

For younger students, a splash of pictures exercises the same cognitive function.

Students predict elements of the story and search for connections between ideas in the illustrations. One way to create the splashes is to purchase a paperback copy of the selected text and cut out the pictures. Another way is to photocopy some or all of the illustrations to create the splash for small groups of students to sort and sequence. These picture sets then make excellent cues for student retelling of the story.

The Whooping Cranes' Story

dance small fish *extinct*

endangered species 1940s

New Mexico two eggs

foster parents

filled in marsh plants

Canada Aransas

accidentally shot

Variations:

- The same procedure can be followed for a lecture, demonstration or audiovisual presentation, interspersing the Word Splash process by pausing periodically for students to examine their statements.

- Another option is to give groups or individuals copies of the splash on which to record their statements.

- Once students are familiar with the strategy, they can create their own word splashes. Used in this manner, the strategy becomes an organizing and integrating exercise. This process can also be used as a form of alternative assessment.

3

-
-
-

2

-
-
-

1

-

'h to students' learning logs or journals. At the end of ng an audio visual presentation, or even after a field :pond in writing with a 3 - 2 - 1 structure.

for success in writing. Asking learners for six pieces 2vable and gives students a sense of accomplishment

haracter

OR

ative writing

Variations:

• The **3-2-1** format can be easily adapted for activating ind engaging. Before being introduced to a new topic, viewing a demonstration or reading a piece of literature, /ou can assign a **3-2-1** writing task. For example, you might ask students for **3** things they know about the topic, **2** predictions and **1** thing they're looking forward to.

• You can ask students about their own learning, or their group processes using **3-2-1.** For example, **3** strategies you used during this activity, **2** things you noticed about your own thinking, **1** thing you might do differently next time.

2 things you would like to know more about

1 idea that you will write about tonight

• Students often enjoy sharing their log entries with their peers. The logs make ideal vehicles for small-group discussions. The **3-2-1** gives the group work a specific focus and facilitates sharing. It gives students the opportunity to share successful learning strategies or particularly difficult concepts and ways to understand them.

• **3-2-1 plus 1:**
Each student creates his or her own 3-2-1 sheet. Students share their individual work with a small table group. As they listen to each other, group members place additional items in their +1 columns. This variation reinforces listening skills and enhances the group's knowledge base.

• 3-2-1 plus 1 can be coupled with the Focused Reading Strategy (page 63) as a powerful comprehension builder.

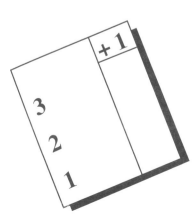

A⃞ See Page 104

Say Something

Say Something *is a paired reading strategy developed by Jerome Harste for constructing meaning from text-based information. Through structured exchanges, partners develop relationships between new information and what they already know or believe. Thinking out loud, supported by attentive listening, increases individual and shared understanding.*

Directions:

1. Partners read silently to a designated stopping point. When both students are ready, they each have a turn to "say something" about what they have just read.

   The 'something' might be a question, a brief summary, a key point, an interesting idea or a new connection.

2. Once they have reached a designated stopping point and have each had an opportunity to "say something", the process continues. Students read to the next stopping point, and so on, until the selection is completed.

3. Once all students are ready (or after a predetermined time period), the class engages in a discussion of the text.

Variation

Key Concepts / Key Ideas *is a variation of Say Something. In this version, partners first work on their own, identifying what they believe are some key concepts and key ideas in the text. This method encourages individual thinking and provides peer support.*

Directions:

1. Establish learning pairs.

2. Each partner reads the selection silently, highlighting words or short phrases that capture important or interesting ideas.

3. Once both partners have read through and marked their text, they share and discuss highlighted items, taking turns initiating an idea for exploration.

4. After a designated amount of time, open the discussion to the entire class by having partners share some of their new thinking and questions.

The First Word

The First Word is a variation on traditional acrostics. To activate student thinking, place the name of a topic or a key concept vertically down the side of a page. Working in small groups or on their own, students generate a short phrase or sentence that begins with each letter of the vertical word and offers important information or key characteristics about the topic.

Sun is the star at the center of the solar system.

Orbits are the paths that planets take around the Sun.

Lunar eclipses occur when the Moon gets blocked by the Earth.

Asteroids are big rocks that orbit the Sun.

Rings—the planet Saturn has them.

Saturn is the sixth planet from the Sun.

You can see some planets with your naked eye.

Some other planets are: Earth, Venus, Mars, Jupiter, Pluto, and Neptune.

The Earth is the only planet with life on it.

Every year, the Earth orbits the Sun once.

Mercury is the planet closest to the Sun.

When students have completed their first drafts, they should check them over to see if they have left out any essential ideas.

This structure taps language arts skills as much as it does content knowledge. Those differences can be a useful criteria for structuring teams for this activity. Students with strong language skills can be mixed with those who have ready content knowledge.

The Last Word

The First Word *can also be used at the end of a lesson or unit. Used in this manner, it is called the **Last Word**. The* Last Word *can be used as a means of processing for understanding and as an alternative assessment device. Here are some examples of the* Last Word *in action, showing a variety of content applications. There are many possibilities beyond the ones here.*

Plants make their own food.
Hairs on the roots aid absorption.
Only takes place in the presence of light.
This is an important process that takes place in green leaves.
Oxygen is produced.
Synthesis means "to make."
You need plants for food.
Nutrients are absorbed.
Tubes transport nutrients.
Has a need for chlorophyll.
Energy comes from the sun.
Sugar is a by-product.
In photosynthesis carbon dioxide is necessary.
Stomates are found in leaves.

Developed with Monica Burress, Dorothy Caruolo, John Cooley and Phyllis Mickish, Peekskill Middle School, Peekskill, New York.

Depends on voters' participation.
Equitable application of the law.
Modeled on the Greeks.
Offers equal opportunity to all.
Citizens share responsibilities and rights.
Rights are guaranteed under the law.
Attains civil liberties for all.
Change is accomplished in an orderly way.
Your voice counts in yearly elections.

Source: M. Buckley, Yorktown, NY

*Here is a wonderful variation of the **Last Word** strategy developed by grade seven teacher Elizabeth Sorrell as a review for a unit on the skeletal system. Students wrote the title in the following way before watching a filmstrip on the topic.*

After viewing the filmstrip, students were challenged to use the words and ideas they had learned in the unit and in the filmstrip to fill in the word puzzle. The goal was to assign terms and ideas to the correct column, choosing whether the idea applied to the structure or function of the skeletal system. Students were awarded one point for each correct answer, two points if no one else had the same idea.

Structures	Functions
T-	**T-**
Haversian Canals	**H -**
E -	Exercise muscles
Scapula	Support
Knee - cap	**K -**
E -	**E -**
L -	**L -**
E -	**E -**
Tendons	**T -**
A -	Attachment of muscles
Ligament	Levers
S -	**S -**
Yellow Marrow	**Y -**
S -	**S -**
Tarsals	**T -**
E -	**E -**
Metacarpals	Maker of cells

CHAPTER 3

PATTERNS & PRACTICES:
Mediating Student Thinking

A LL *students' eyes are riveted on the glass of water in the teacher's right hand and the coffee cup in her left. She sips dramatically from the glass, demonstrating that this liquid is safe to drink. Smiling, she carefully pours the remaining contents of the glass into the coffee cup. The students gasp as she raises her arm and inverts the cup in mid-air. To their surprise no liquid escapes! Their silence becomes a buzz of interaction as they excitedly share their amazement and try to explain this surprising turn of events.*

The teacher refocuses their attention and begins inquiring: "What do you think might be going on here?"

Seeking meaning through inquiry and interaction are hallmarks in the learning-focused classroom. If students are to develop identities as thinkers and problem solvers, then teachers must also develop and expand their identities as mediators of meaning-making.

Patterns & Practices: Mediating Student Thinking

In its Latin roots, *mediate* means "in the middle." In the learning-focused classroom, the teacher occupies a position in the middle of students, materials and ideas. Here the role is to strategically focus students' attention on both content and process. Through the tools of questioning and paraphrasing, the mediational teacher provides a focus and an emotional and cognitive support system for student thinking. While there is much research on teacher questioning, there is little certainty as to a precise prescription for success. What is emerging, though, are patterns of interaction in which teachers are conduits and facilitators of thinking rather than inquisitors in control of the subject and pace of instructional events.

The mediational flow we recommend follows this pattern:

1. The teacher presents a well-framed question. (See details on following pages.)

2. There is a collective pause of 3–5 seconds.

3. Someone responds.

4. There is a second collective pause of 3–5 seconds.

5. The student who initially answered often elaborates when given additional "think-time."

6. The teacher or a student paraphrases the first student's response. (See details on following pages.)

7. The teacher or student who paraphrased inquires for details to support the initial position or inquires to extend the thinking.

8. The first student elaborates and other students join in.

9. The pattern continues.

The extensive classroom research of Mary Budd Rowe and the rich work of Arthur Costa and Reuven Feuerstein strongly supports this basic template. As students' confidence with this discourse practice increases, they learn to trust their own and others' thinking processes. In this way, true learning communities emerge.

Mediational teachers draw from two important knowledge bases. One is their own knowledge of the content at hand. The other is knowledge of mediation itself. These resources work hand-in-hand. Neither by itself is sufficient. Knowing what to ask without knowing how and when to ask can lead to confusion and misconceptions. Knowing how to ask without attention to the accuracy of content knowledge can also confuse and direct student attention away from important concepts and understandings.

Well-crafted questions initially match the database that students have access to, either internally or externally. They build a foundation for collective knowledge upon which the class can firmly anchor thoughts and speculations.

Thoughtful paraphrases support this construction and connect students to their own ideas and to the ideas of others. The ratio of paraphrases to questions is one thing to notice in the classrooms of teachers who build strong cognitive communities. A second thing to notice is the rhythm and flow of the questioning, pausing and paraphrasing pattern.

Who asks the questions is another critical element. The questioning and paraphrasing templates we offer here are for student use as much as teacher use. It is often more productive to have students develop questions about material and ideas than to have them respond to teacher or textbook-generated questions.

The intention to understand ideas and one another is the root of all work on questioning and paraphrasing. This intention drives the essential need for attending fully and listening carefully. This communication basic is best taught to students by modeling. Curious teachers who listen and inquire develop these same habits in others. Pattern is the ultimate teacher, not isolated technique.

A Template for Questions

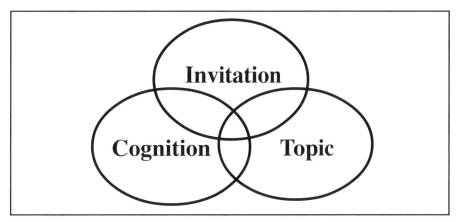

Well-crafted questions combine three essential elements: an *invitation* to engage and think, a *topic* to think about, and a *cognitive focus* for how to think about the topic. These elements can be combined in a variety of ways and do not always appear in the same order. Personal style and the matter at hand both play a part in this construction.

COGNITIVE WORD BANK

ACTIVATING
Recall, name, tell, match, count, notice, describe, select, observe

EXPLORING
Sort, classify, reason, explain, infer, contrast, compare, distinguish, analyze, weigh

INTEGRATING
Evaluate, speculate, predict, estimate, imagine, forecast, deduce, suppose, induce, postulate, hypothesize, theorize, conclude, suppose

The Invitation

The invitation to think comes from the following elements.

1. The use of an approachable voice. The skilled observer and teacher Michael Grinder notes that this voice is well modulated and ends on a rising inflection.

2. The use of plural forms. Instead of asking *"What is a* reason *for...?"*, ask *"What are some* reasons *for...?"* Plural forms signal that there is more than one possible right answer.

3. The use of exploratory language. Using words such as *might, some* and *could be* signals that there are multiple possible responses, not one right answer. Avoiding stems such as *have you, can you, do you*, invites elaboration, not a yes or no response.
   "What are some possible explanations?"
   "What are your hunches about . . . ?"
   "What might be the causes of . . . ?"

4. The use of open-ended forms. These questions are non-dichotomous and can not be answered yes or no. Eliminate starters like; *"Have you . . . ?"*, *"Can you . . . ?"* or *"Did you . . . ?"*.

5. **The use of positive presuppositions.** This language form presupposes capacity and willingness to engage. Instead of asking, *"Can anyone tell me if ..."* or *"Does anyone know the answer to . . . ?"* you might say, *"As you examine the data table, what are some of the details that you are noticing?"* or *"Reflect for a minute on the following—and compare your thinking today to your thinking about this topic last week. What are some of the similarities and differences that are emerging?"*

Cognition

A targeted verb establishes the cognitive focus of a question. Well-chosen verbs combined with an invitation to think and an engaging topic effectively frame the personal and collective intellectual task. Each phase in the teaching/learning cycle structures specific cognition. We urge you to develop your own word banks to cue this thinking for yourself and for your students.

A Template for Paraphrasing

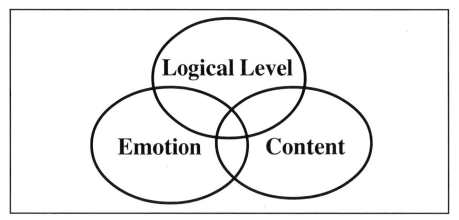

Mediational paraphrases contain three important elements; they label the speaker's *content*, the speaker's *emotions* about the content and frame a *logical level* for holding the content. Skilled paraphrasing treats student responses as gifts. The paraphrase reflects that student's thinking back to the student for further consideration and connects that response to the flow of discourse emerging within the group. Paraphrasing also creates permission to inquire for details and elaboration. Without the paraphrase, students may perceive such inquiries as interrogation.

Mediational paraphrases establish a relationship between people and ideas. Well-crafted paraphrasing with appropriate pausing triggers more thoughtful responses than asking questions alone. It aligns the speaker and responder, placing both on an equal footing. Questioning, no matter how skillful and nonthreatening in appearance, distances by degrees the asker from the asked. The paraphrase creates a safe environment within which to think.

Mediational paraphrasing is a process with structure and flow. It is driven by the:
1. intention to support thinking and problem solving.
2. attention of the paraphraser, who listens fully for the essence of the message
3. linguistic skills of the paraphraser

Structure

• **Listen** to calibrate the content and emotions of the speaker.

• **Signal** that you are about to paraphrase.

We signal our intention by modulating our intonation, using an approachable voice and by opening with a reflective stem. Such stems put the emphasis and focus on the initial speaker's words, not on the paraphraser's interpretation of those words. As a general rule of thumb, reflective paraphrases do not contain the pronoun "I." We are actively campaigning to abolish the paraphrase stem, *"What I think I hear you saying . . . "* This overused form signals to many listeners that their thoughts no longer matter and that the paraphraser is now going to insert his or her own ideas into the conversation instead of reflecting the thinking and feeling of the initial speaker.

Flow

Choose a logical level with which to respond.
1. **Acknowledge and clarify.** If you are not completely accurate the speaker will offer corrections. *"So, this reading*

Paraphrase Signals

You're noticing . . .
As you consider . . .
You're suggesting . . .
You're thinking . . .
You're wondering . . .
You're excited
  about . . .
So, you are
  speculating that . . .
So, your hunch
  is . . .
You've observed
  that . . .

For global thinkers, summary paraphrases that separate and organize thinking-in-progress are a real gift. At other times, shifting the level of abstraction down grounds their thinking in specific examples and details.

For those who think in highly sequential and concrete patterns, the shift up to a higher logical level helps them to explore a bigger picture and provides a wider context for thinking.

passage makes you feel sad because it reminds you of something similar that happened to you."

2. **Summarize and organize** by offering themes and containers which organize the statement or separate jumbled issues. *"You're noticing two issues here, they are . . . " "You're describing three tasks, then. First you'll, then . . . and finally, . . . " "You have a need then to clarify two things, what you want to have happen and how to make it happen."*

3. **Shift level of abstraction to a higher or lower level**. Paraphrases often move through a pattern of acknowledging, then summarizing, then shifting focus to a higher or lower logical level.

We move to higher logical levels from the concrete by using paraphrases that name concepts, themes, goals and values. *"So, you see this as another example of the negative impact of the global economy." "You're suggesting that these might all fit into a larger category called...." "So, what you most value here is...."*

We move to lower logical levels when abstractions and concepts need grounding in details. *"An example of an ecosystem then might be found in our own classroom aquarium." "Given that big idea about democracy, our school election might be an example of those principles in action."*

Paraphrasing works hand-in-hand with questioning and pausing to establish and support an environment for thinking. These are vital teaching skills that make a difference for student learning in all content areas. They are also important communication skills for our students to master. Daily immerson in cognitively rich surroundings in which these patterns are modeled, taught and reinforced instills the listening and speaking skills for academic success.

Paraphrase Examples

Student: "I think the United States and Canada are alike in many ways. People drive the same cars, they listen to the same music and watch the same movies."

Teacher: "You're aware of several similarities between the two countries."
(Acknowledge and or clarify)

Teacher: "You're naming parallels in several areas; automobiles, popular music and movie viewing habits."
(Summarize and organize)

Teacher: "So, you are noticing similar lifestyle patterns in the two countries."
(Shift level of abstraction up a logical level to a broader category label)

The teacher or another student can now inquire about other similarities between the two countries or move to exploring some of the differences.

Silence

- After the teacher asks a question
- After the student gives an answer
- After the student asks a question

Paraphrasing

Three Types of Paraphrases

1. Acknowledge and clarify—calibrating content and emotions

2. Summarize and organize—a statement of themes, big ideas and separation of confusing and/or jumbled issues

3. Shift level of abstraction—a shift in logical level, either up to a category or conceptual level or down to a concrete example

Verbal Response Behaviors

- **Silence**
- **Paraphrasing**
- **Accepting**
- **Clarifying**
- **Extending**

Accepting

Without value judgments

1. Passively
2. Actively
3. Empathically

Clarifying

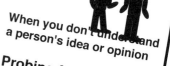

When you don't understand a person's idea or opinion

Probing for Specificity

- Who
- What
- Why
- Where
- When
- How

Extending

Making data available when the student is in need

1. Giving information
2. Sending "I" messages
3. Providing resources

Based on the work of Arthur L. Costa

Praise and Feedback

Praise and feedback are not the same thing. Global praise does not let students know which aspects of their performance meet expectations or standards. Unspecific praise is usually used to build relationships with students and to express overall pleasure with the behavior of a group or of an individual. Such praise works for some students but not for others. In fact, students' response to teacher praise can vary from highly positive through neutral to highly negative. Praise will act as a reinforcement for some students, but other students will be indifferent to it and still other students will actually experience it as punishment. This is especially true for task-focused students and gifted students who are intrinsically motivated. These students have their own standards for success. It is better to coach them to help them clarify their own standards than to try to impose our own measures of excellence.

Rather than just assume the effectiveness of praise, teachers should monitor students for their reaction to it and respond accordingly.

Effective praise is specific, well timed and matched to the individual or group. Such praise provides detailed feedback about products and performances. It is:

1. **Specific**, providing focused and accurate comments about work and actions.

2. **Contingent,** based upon actual accomplishment, not generalized possibilities.

3. **Genuine**, showing a variety of responses and not simply drawing from a menu of pet phrases.

4. **Congruent,** offered as close as possible to the actual praiseworthy event or accomplishment.

5. **Appropriate,** geared to the level of accomplishment and matched to the personality of the receiver.

Effective Praise:

- **Specific**
- **Contingent**
- **Genuine**
- **Congruent**
- **Appropriate**

Existing theory and data suggests that the following types of students may respond positively to well-constructed praise:

1. Early-grade students—especially those oriented towards pleasing adults

2. Low-performing students —especially early grades

3. Students from low socioeconomic backgrounds

4. Minority students

5. Introverts

6. Individuals with an external locus of control

7. Field-dependent individuals (oriented toward relationship, not task)

Jere Brophy (1981)

Wait Time

In many classrooms the teacher dominates the interactions using a rapid-fire pace and lower cognitive level questions. Teachers typically wait less than 1 second after posing a question before doing one of several things: repeating the question, commenting on a student answer, redirecting the question to a new student, answering the question themselves or starting a new questioning sequence. Students' answers are often terse, fragmentary or show a lack of confidence with inflected tones.

After a student replies, many teachers again wait less than 1 second before commenting or asking another question. There is little chance for students to have second thoughts or to extend their ideas. Many teachers appear to be programmed to accept one predetermined "right" answer. There is little room left for alternative answers or differing opinions. The message students receive is that the teacher's way of knowing is the only way of knowing.

Research History

The concept of wait time was first developed by the noted science educator, Dr. Mary Budd Rowe, in the late 1960s. In observing classrooms where the Science Curriculum Improvement Study (SCIS) program was being tested, she noticed that some teachers were using pauses purposefully as they conducted lessons and class discussions. In these classrooms she noted students speculating, holding sustained conversational sequences, posing alternative explanations and arguing over the interpretation of data.

Dr. Rowe noted the following ripple effects of these pauses:

1. Positive changes in affective climate.
2. Positive changes in the quality of classroom interactions.
3. An increased level of cognitive functioning (Bloom's Taxonomy).
4. An increased level of academic achievement.
5. A decreased number of behavior problems.

Wait Time Defined

Mary Budd Rowe defined two types of wait time: **Wait Time I** is the length of time a teacher pauses after asking a question; **Wait Time II** is the length of time a teacher waits after a student comments or asks a question. A minimum of three seconds of pausing is recommended. With higher level cognitive tasks, 5 seconds or more of wait time may be required to achieve positive results.

We have added **Wait Time III**, or the length of time a teacher takes before responding to a student's question. This type of pause communicates thoughtfulness, value for the question and the importance of thinking before responding.

10-2

The use of longer pauses in whole group lecture settings has also been examined by Dr. Rowe. Students need mental processing time in information dense subjects like chemistry, physics and geology. Her research indicates that retention and understanding increase when two to three minutes of discussion, note clarification and question raising with seatmates are provided after every eight to ten minutes of instruction. All unresolved student questions are reserved for the last five minutes of the class. She calls this pattern **10-2** time (see p. 62).

Learning to Control Wait Time

Learning to monitor and control wait time takes patience and some effort. Tape-recording lessons and transcribing them with watch in hand is an effective means

Wait Time

Wait Time I
After the teacher
asks a question

Wait Time II
After a student
responds

Wait Time III
Before the teacher
responds to a
student

of gaining insight into your own teaching. This method does not interrupt the flow of the lesson and allows you to monitor your language use, pacing and the cognitive level of your questions. Having a colleague observe you and give feedback is another means of increasing wait time. In either case be sure to let your students know what's up. They will notice the change in the operation of the class and can be enlisted to help you monitor the wait time you provide them and the wait time they provide you and each other.

Metacognition

Skilled thinkers monitor and control their thinking while they are thinking. This process, called metacognition, is the hallmark of skilled thinkers, problem solvers and decision makers across all arenas of life and learning. The prefix *meta* means "above" or "beyond." In practical terms it means focusing students on both the thinking and their own "thinking about their thinking" as they engage in tasks and activities.

In a math lesson, this might mean asking students to describe the strategies they used in a problem-solving activity and recording these on a chart. In future lessons, students could then label the strategies they used and add to the list as a way of expanding their repertoires of problem-solving skills. In these types of lessons, the focus is on both the thinking and inner dialogue of the thinker. The teacher might ask, *"What do you say to yourself when you get stuck?" or "How do you know when you are confused or off-track?"*

Classroom Changes With Increased Wait Time

1. 300%–700% increase in the length of student responses.
2. The number of unsolicited but appropriate responses increases.
3. Failures to respond decrease.
4. Confidence increases—there are fewer inflected responses.
5. Speculative responses increase.
6. Teacher-centered show-and-tell decreases—student-to-student interaction increases.
7. Teacher questions change in number and kind.
   - The number of divergent questions increases
   - Teachers ask higher level questions (Bloom's Taxonomy)
   - There is more probing for clarification
8. Students make inferences and support inferences with data.
9. Students ask more questions.
10. Contributions by "slow" students increase.
11. Disciplinary moves decrease—more students are on task.
12. Achievement on logic tests improves.

Metacognitive processing can be built into a content reading assignment by using the Focused Reading strategy. Students mark text with the following symbols to indicate their level of understanding and connection making.

Focused Reading

✔ Got it. I know and/or understand this.

! This is really important or interesting.

? I don't understand this or this does not make sense.

Active engagement with text in this way supports content, concept and reading skills development. After reading, student teams gather to compare their responses. They might also use the 3-2-1 strategy as a response mechanism by sharing **3 ✔'s, 2!'s** and **1?** with the whole class (see p. 43).

Researchers, Margaret Wang, Geneva Haertel and Herbert Walberg make the persuasive claim that teaching students cognitive and metacognitive strategies is the most influential aspect of academic success. Their analysis of multiple research studies places these teachable and learnable skills above home environment in degree of impact on learning.

Metacognition has two important aspects, *self-regulation* or knowledge and control of the self and *process monitoring* or knowledge and control of thinking processes. Robert Marzano and his co-authors describe these aspects as follows:

Self-regulation

1. **Monitoring and controlling commitment.** Commitment is a choice learners make. It can be directed and controlled. It is not the same as our feelings about the task or project. With consciousness and discipline we commit to the work whether we enjoy it in the moment or not.

2. **Monitoring and controlling attitudes.** Attitudes are closely related to commitment. Attitudes, emotions and actions mutually influence one another. Social theorist Bernard Weiner, in his noted work on attribution theory, points to the powerful message that effort pays off. Focused effort is at its heart a matter of attitude.

3. **Monitoring and controlling attention.** Human attention comes in two forms, the automatic and the voluntary. The human brain is wired to notice novelty and pattern interruption. Sudden noises and movement attract our senses and pull our focus from the task at hand. We have control over voluntary attention. We choose to sit up straight, to listen carefully, to note details and patterns and to read carefully.

Process Monitoring

Monitoring and controlling thinking processes has two important elements. The first is awareness of the types of knowledge important in cognition and metacognition. The second is exercising executive control of behavior.

Types of Knowledge

1. **Declarative knowledge.** This level of information is factual knowledge that can be recalled as needed. Multiplication facts, the elements of the periodic table and key dates and events in World War II are all examples of declarative knowledge.

2. **Procedural knowledge.** This type of knowledge means knowing how to do something. Predicting, inferring and distinguishing fact from opinion are all examples of procedural knowledge involved in reading comprehension. Knowing how to multiply three digit numbers by two digit numbers is an example of mathematical procedural knowledge.

3. **Conditional knowledge.** This degree of understanding means knowing when to do something and why it does or does not work in that setting. Skilled thinkers and problem solvers strategically draw from a repertoire of strategies and apply them conditionally. In practice this might mean knowing a variety of mathematical problem-solving strategies such as working the problem backwards or representing it with manipulatives and diagrams. In reading, it means knowing when to skim for essence and when to search for details and supporting facts.

Executive Control of Behavior

Confident learners exercise executive control over their thinking. This essential metacognitive function operates like a thermostat or temperature gauge to monitor and regulate attention, cognitive processes and progress towards goals. Noted thinking skills proponent Barry Beyer proposes a three-phase model for this aspect of metacognition.

1. **Planning**

   - Stating a goal
   - Selecting operations to perform
   - Sequencing operations
   - Identifying potential obstacles and errors
   - Predicting results desired and/or anticipated

2. **Monitoring**

   - Keeping the goal in mind
   - Keeping one's place in a sequence
   - Knowing when a subgoal has been achieved
   - Deciding when to go on to the next operation
   - Selecting the next appropriate operation
   - Spotting errors or obstacles
   - Knowing how to recover from errors and overcome obstacles

3. **Assessing**

   - Assessing goal achievement
   - Judging the accuracy and adequacy of results
   - Evaluating the appropriateness of procedures used
   - Assessing the handling of obstacles and errors
   - Judging the efficiency of the plan and its execution

Metacognition does not happen automatically. It results from explicit, context-based teaching and modeling. Across content and social domains, effective teachers design lessons that demonstrate and reinforce the thinking and meta-thinking strategies embedded in academic tasks and in deep understanding of important knowledge and skills.

Graphic Organizers

Graphic organizers visually represent and display concepts and information. With practice and mastery, they become thinking tools and memory support systems for learners of all ages.

Creating graphic organizers helps students to select important ideas and relationships from the mass of details they encounter in text, lectures, notes and multimedia materials. Finished graphic organizers make pictures in the mind for confident storage and easy retrieval.

Since the majority of students are kinesthetically and or visually dominant thinkers, developing and using graphic organizers becomes an important lifelong learning skill.

During the Activating and Engaging phase, many different graphic organizers can be used to surface prior knowledge. Semantic maps, Venn diagrams, grids and matrices are all useful for helping students display existing knowledge and organizational schemes. Later in the unit, these early exhibits become touchstones for marking progress and comparing and contrasting what is now known with what was first known.

In the Exploring and Discovering phase, graphic organizers are prime thinking and reasoning tools for sorting out relationships and extracting and isolating the essence of a topic. Cause-and-effect maps, cycle graphics and chain of events diagrams are all examples of such tools for thinking. This phase extends to work done outside of class. When students have mastery of the tools and can apply graphic organizers independently, they become excellent study tools. This is especially true when students are reading in the content areas and working with textbooks.

When learning moves to the Organizing and Integrating phase, graphic organizers have tremendous impact on conceptual development, information synthesis and summarization. Many of the same graphic devices used during the earlier phases can be revisited here to be polished into final detailed form. It is an easy transition from the Organizing and Integrating phase to the assessment of learning. Graphic organizers make excellent assessment devices for content in

---

To develop confident and independent use of graphic organizers:

1. Introduce graphic organizers one at a time using concrete examples from current or familiar material.

2. Describe the purpose and graphic structure of the tool. Point out the type of thinking this organizer supports.

3. Model the graphic development of the organizer with a scaled-down version of the tool.

4. Guide student practice with material that has been previously mastered.

5. Collaboratively develop a version using new material. Challenge students to do as much of the thinking as possible. Have students copy the completed sample into their notebooks.

6. Present multiple opportunities to practice each tool.

7. As students develop their tool kits, select material and have students choose the most appropriate graphic organizer to display the type of thinking and understanding the content requires.

8. Continue exploring the cognitive and metacognitive strategies involved with using these tools as new applications develop.

which understanding relationships, not just recall of details, is important.

The real power of graphic organizers becomes clear when students have mastered their use and can independently apply them to learning tasks. They are sophisticated additions to all learners' tool kits. It takes careful planning and thoughtful instruction to help students learn to use and correctly employ these tools.

Phases of Thinking

An attention to thinking organizes the three-phase model described in Chapter Two. This focus is what turns the resources in this book into strategies and not just activities. The goal in activity planning is to engage student attention and occupy time. Student involvement and enjoyment are the usual measures of success. The goal of strategy thinking is to simultaneously engage students with important knowledge and skills and to help them develop a bank of thinking strategies and habits of mind to apply to future lessons.

We can use the Focused Reading strategy described above as a simple accountability device. We can also use it as the centerpiece of a deeper inquiry into why and how students know what they know and feel what they feel. Instead of monitoring for compliance with the structure, we can probe into student responses. *"How are some of the ways that you know that?"* or *"What are some of your reasons for marking that passage with an exclamation point?"* or *"How might you go about sorting that question out?"*

The first phase of the model, Activating and Engaging, supports the generation of ideas. It is here that we connect students to the territory we are exploring or about to explore. Prior knowledge and skills emerge as we surface and organize what is known and not known. The planning phase of metacognition comes into play as students set goals and make predictions about the journey ahead. This is especially important in reading and writing and problem-solving tasks of all types.

The second phase,   , applies active thinking strategies to the processing of information, ideas and experiences. Careful observation and description of the details in text and physical materials organizes this phase. Resourceful learners draw upon their metacognitive repertoire by carefully monitoring where they are in the process and how they are progressing towards goal accomplishment. In a science lab, they keep the essential inquiry question in mind as they manipulate materials and tools. They might ask themselves questions like, *"How accurate do we need to be when taking these measurements?"* or *"How should we display this data?"* and *"What tentative conclusions are we drawing and what data supports these conclusions?"*

The third phase, Organizing and Integrating, helps students synthesize their current understandings at this stage of the learning. By writing, drawing and using graphic organizers, students pull together images for themselves of the ideas and concepts they are developing. Reflection on process and goal achievement is another feature of this phase. Both successes and mistakes, when noted and understood, contribute to future learning. Without such processing, mistakes are likely to be repeated and successes may become flukes and not consistent patterns.

GRAPHIC ORGANIZERS

Graphic organizers are thinking tools and memory supports for processing events, information and relationships. They help students to:

1. Select and describe

2. Clarify and explain

3. Sort and organize

Strategies for Mediating Thinking

*The **10-2** structure was developed by the noted science educator, Dr. Mary Budd Rowe, to allow students time to process information and concepts during large-group instruction.*

In the 10-2 structure, teachers provide input or students engage with materials for 10 minutes, followed by a 2-minute pause. During the pause, student partners or teams share their notes, fill in gaps in their own notes, and help each other clarify concepts. Students usually are not allowed to ask the teacher questions during these pauses. This rule builds interdependence among teams, causing students to rely on one another for help instead of assuming that the teacher will bail them out.

Unresolved questions and issues are reserved for the last 5 minutes of the period. During this time, the class interacts to sort out misconceptions and gaps in data or logic.

Note: 10-2 is not a precise formula. It is a ratio of input to process time. The time structures can be varied, depending on student dynamics and the complexity of the material being presented.

Variations:

• This strategy works well with audiovisual presentations. Be sure to preview materials carefully to identify logical pausing points.

• Structure the interaction during the pause. For example; ask pairs or teams to summarize key points, define particular terms, or make connections between the new material and their own experiences.

Focused Reading

Focused Reading *promotes active engagement with text. It encourages students to think while they read and to compare and contrast their current knowledge with the information that they are encountering in new material. It is an excellent strategy for both in-class and homework reading assignments.*

Directions:

1. Introduce students to the focused reading symbols. ✔ = Got it. I know or understand this. ! = This is really important or interesting. ? = I don't understand this or this does not make sense.

2. Assign a text passage for reading and marking with the three symbols. Using photocopied text for early trials of this strategy allows students to mark right on the paper. Later they can transfer the symbols to notes they keep while reading textbooks and other printed materials they cannot write on.

3. After reading, student teams of three to four students gather to compare their responses.

4. Student teams select sample items from each category to share with the class

Variations:

- Have student teams use the 3-2-1 strategy to organize their sharing.
  They select 3 ✔'s, 2 !'s and 1? to share. Responses can be put on charts for visual display.

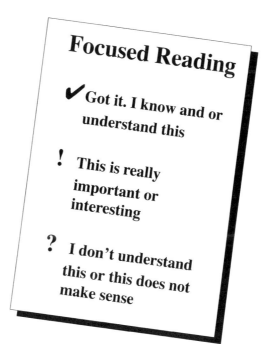

Focused Reading

✔ Got it. I know and or understand this

! This is really important or interesting

? I don't understand this or this does not make sense

Chain of Events Diagrams

Chain of Events Diagrams *show the sequences of events or processes that flow towards a final outcome. They are a process scaffold for sequential thinking. They can be used to display organic processes, events in nature and events in stories. They are excellent story summarizers and they provide wonderful planning structures for writing. Used in this way, they become graphic guides for writing both fiction and nonfiction.*

Directions:

1. Introduce students to one of the two graphic forms for chain of event diagrams.
2. Supply student teams with a blank graphic and with details to a known process like making a sandwich.
3. Have the teams sequence the events and or actions, placing them in the proper position within the graphic.
4. Introduce a new topic area from content with which you are working.
5. Have student teams apply the organizer to this new content.

Activate and *Engage* by brainstorming events during a period of time (from when you wake up until you leave for school).

Then have students sequence using chain of events map.

Event 1	First _____ happened.
Event 2	Then _____ happened.
Event 3	Followed by _____.
Final Outcome	Finally _____.

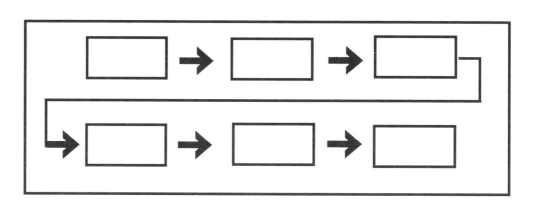

Cycle Diagrams

Cycle Diagrams *show the flow of events and sequences that are cyclical in nature. They are excellent for displaying the stages and phases of processes in science and social studies content. Cycle Diagrams visually emphasize the return to the beginning stage. The transition between the four seasons is a simple example of this idea.*

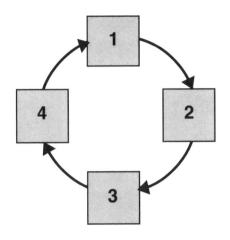

Here are some examples of Cycle Diagrams in use.

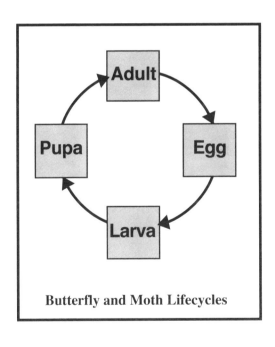

Butterfly and Moth Lifecycles

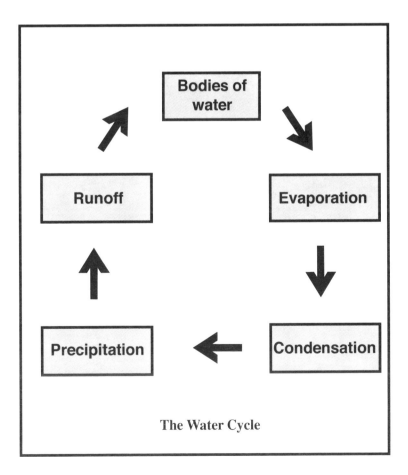

The Water Cycle

Network Trees

Network Trees *display a hierarchy of ideas. They are especially useful for articulating concepts and supporting details in descending order of importance. Many concepts and themes in all content areas lend themselves to this form of organization.*

Network Trees support the cognitive skills of classifying and categorizing. As a process scaffold, they focus and reinforce this critical thinking skill.

Directions:

1. Write a concept high on the board and draw an oval around it.

2. Draw two parallel ovals below the first and label them with the names of major categories.

3. Draw parallel ovals below each of the categories to supply examples and details.

4. Add further rows of ovals to refine the details and provide concrete examples.

Variations:

- To scaffold learning, provide premade graphic forms with the concept and categories in place. Have students provide supporting details.

- Provide students with premade graphic forms with a set number of slots to be filled in for both categories and details.

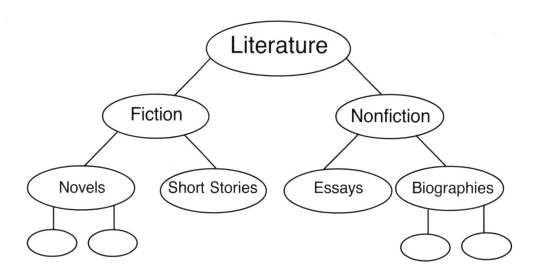

Spider Diagrams

Spider Diagrams *illuminate main ideas and supporting details within topic theme. They help learners sort out hierarchies within topics and separate major themes from finer points. Like other graphic organizers, Spider Diagrams are useful for activating and engaging prior knowledge and as prewriting scaffolds.*

Directions:

1. Write a topic theme on the board and draw a circle around it.

2. Draw three to four branches and label them with main ideas.

3. Ask students to provide supporting details to flesh out the main ideas.

4. Add other main ideas if students think of details that do not fit with the existing main ideas.

Variations:

• Have pairs or trios create their own Spider Diagrams.

• To scaffold learning, provide premade graphic forms with the main ideas in place. Have students provide supporting details.

• Provide students with premade graphic forms with a set number of slots to be filled in for both main ideas and details.

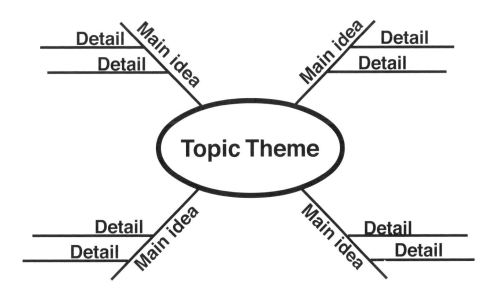

Compare/Contrast Matrix

A Compare/Contrast Matrix *displays details in an organized way so that they can be compared across examples. Visually containing elements in a matrix supports students in learning key features of a category and helps them to see how examples are alike and how they are different.*

Directions:

1. On a chart or overhead transparency, display the matrix with the categories labeled.

2. Fill in one row using an example with which students are familiar.

3. Using other familiar examples, have students join you in filling out the rest of the sample chart.

4. Give students blank charts to fill in new examples for the topic you are exploring.

Variations:

- With a new topic, have students generate the categories for comparison.

- Provide students with premade graphic forms. Supply some categories but leave others blank for students to generate.

	Setting	Problem	Character(s)	Style	Genre	Author
Book 1						
Book 2						
Book 3						
Book 4						

Venn Diagrams

Venn Diagrams are one of the most useful and classic graphic organizers. They provide a visual display of similar and different attributes that can be used to launch discussion, writing or further research. They are particularly effective products scaffold for the compare/contrast essays required for content area assessments.

Use Venn Diagrams to compare and contrast:

Ecosystems

A book with a movie

Characters in a play

The same place at different times in history

Geometric figures

Directions:

1. Draw two overlapping circles on the board. Label each side with the name of one of the things you are comparing. Start with easy-to-understand items like apples and oranges.
2. Fill in one side with attributes belonging to that item.
3. Fill in the other side with attributes belonging to that item.
4. Now fill in the center area where the two items share attributes.

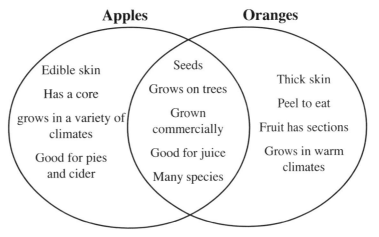

Scaffolding:

Students must be able to hold multiple classification systems in order to cognitively organize the overlapping area of common attributes. For many students, it is useful to provide a scaffold for this complex thinking. As a process scaffold for comparison, first (1) have students fill in a circle of attributes for one of the comparators (e.g., just apples). Then (2) they can fill in a circle of attributes for the other. For the third step, (3) they compare the two items, listing similarities in a long rectangle.

You can also scaffold the process by differentiating between the three sections using color (colored chalk is especially useful for board work).

Variations:

- Venn diagrams can be used to compare three or more items. Students will need to have mastered two item comparisons before moving to this stage.

Learning Logs

Learning Logs *are a simple and straightforward way to help students integrate content, process and personal feelings. They are especially powerful for developing metacognitive processing skills. Learning Logs are an effective method for supporting students' capacity to learn from writing rather than writing what they have learned.*

The most common application of Learning Logs is to have students make entries in their logs during the last 5 minutes of class. Short frequent bursts of writing are more productive over time than are infrequent, longer assignments. You can join in the writing process to reflect on your teaching, note thoughts about your students, preserve anecdotes about their interaction with that day's material and their developing capacities.

To stimulate student thinking, question stems can be written on the board, or kept on a page at the back of their log books. The following types of stems are useful starting points for the learning log process.

- **What are some things I learned today?**
- **What still puzzles me about today's content?**
- **What did I enjoy, hate, accomplish in class today?**
- **What strategies supported my learning?**
- **What did I contribute to others' learning today?**
- **What can I do to enhance my learning in this class?**

Another option is to write four or five key words on the board based on the day's lesson. Ask students to free write about the words for several minutes.

You can collect the logs from time to time, read through them and share written comments with their students. This helps build stronger relationships with students and provides an excellent way to informally assess how well the class is doing.

Getting Started With Learning Logs

ACTIVATING & ENGAGING

- When I think of _____, I think about . . .
- Some things I already know/ think I know about _____
- If I were in _____, I might see/hear _____
- Based on _____, I predict that . . .

EXPLORING & DISCOVERING

- Some ways in which _____ and _____ are both alike are . . .
- Some ways in which _____ and _____ are both different are . . .
- Right now, I think _____ is more important than _____ because . . .
- My sense of _____ tells me that . . .
- Resources I am using now that connect me to this information are . . .
- Some new/other resources I might need are . . .

ORGANIZING & INTEGRATING

- Describe _____ as if you were writing to (fill in role, e.g.: your best friend, someone from another country, your parents)
- If you were going to a birthday party for (a character in a story, a famous person, an historical figure) what kinds of gifts would you bring? Why?
- Redesign _____ to (describe criteria)
- The most difficult thing I am finding about _____ is . . .
- The things that are easiest for me are . . .

METACOGITATING

- I am really pleased about . . .
- One thing I'll change immediately, now that I know what I know . . .
- One thing I would do differently next time . . .
- Some personal implications, connections, insights . . .
- Compare and contrast how you are feeling about this material now and when we began learning about it. (Use a Venn diagram to compare and contrast your confidence with the topic; yourself as a learner, new ways you are thinking about it, etc.)
- Some discoveries I have made today . . .

CHAPTER 4

LEARNING-FOCUSED CLASSROOMS:
Patterns of Interaction

As you enter the classroom, you are surprised to see all the seats empty. Then you spot the students, lined up against the back wall awaiting the teacher's next direction. She instructs the class to organize themselves along the wall according to their opinion on a sensitive issue. As they move to their designated spots, you realize they are forming a human graph! Locations on the line correlate with stances on the issue, pro and con. Each position establishes the degree of agreement or disagreement that student feels.

On any given day, the patterns of student interaction in a learner-centered classroom might shift from direct instruction to paired learning partners to class clusters of three and four students organized around a common interest or assigned task and then back to a full-group activity which has students buzzing around the classroom, then working individually at their seats.

Principles of Interaction

As described throughout this volume, learning occurs on multiple levels and requires multiple means of support. Meaning is constructed both individually and socially. Learners need time to make sense of new information and ideas on their own; they also need time to think aloud and exchange thoughts with others. Frequent opportunities for structured interaction increase students' capacity for learning, develop communication skills and provide practice for important social skills.

A number of variables and design choices influence effective student interaction. Size of group, length of time students stay together as a group, as well as length of time of the activity, use and distribution of materials, and assignment of roles are just a few. This chapter describes a variety of strategies which illustrate these considerations presented in the context of a continuum of interaction.

Of course, the variables involved in designing effective interactions are interrelated. Generally, for example, the shorter the task and/or the smaller the group size, the greater the likelihood for task focus and student success. However, there are a variety of ways to structure for success. You might choose a large group size (four or five students) who collaborate on a task of short duration (20–35 minutes); or you may have students work as partners but stay together as peer editors for an extensive research project. A student's developmental stage and degree of experience working cooperatively, as well as the content area focus, are all important considerations for planning.

Orchestrating group work often requires working slowly at first, to work smoothly and smartly later on. You will need to take the time up front to teach students how to move into groups efficiently, as well as some fundamental skills for working collaboratively. However, preparing students for the complexity of working together productively should not be viewed as down time. Highly structured activities, such as those that follow, have the advantage of engaging students with each other and with important information while supporting efficient transitions and the acquisition of social skills.

Determining Size of Group and Other Considerations for Grouping

Working and learning together productively requires that students have the capacity to successfully manage multiple interactions. Fundamental skills include taking turns, sharing materials and information, and communication skills like using each others' names, paraphrasing and summarizing, and recording accurately and without judgment. Once students are applying these basic skills on a consistent basis, students can exercise more complex

skills, such as shared decision making, consensus building and collaborative inquiry. Setting high expectations for group behavior, and supporting students' success in high-performing groups is an important process in the learning-focused classroom.

To begin the process, you will want to give students lots of experience with paired activities. Once partners are working productively, create activities which require larger groups (i.e., trios and quartets), continuing to add members judiciously. You will also want to shift from quick, interactive strategies to projects which require students to remain as a group over greater periods of time.

Random or Not

Another important consideration is whether groups are teacher created, student created, or selected randomly. There are occasions when you will want to determine the composition of the group, based on academic performance, diversity of student learning styles or background experiences, shared interests, specific need for skill development, etc. Other times, you may want to give students a voice in forming groups. Two important variables in determining grouping decisions are how long the group will remain together and the nature of the task. For example, times when students will be involved in a quick, partnered or trio activity might be good times to offer them choice. If the project will last for several weeks, you might want more control over the composition of the group.

Meet, Greet and Share: Partnered Activities

Partnered activities are the simplest interactions to organize and orchestrate. Yet they are extremely potent. Partnered activities add variety to the instructional day, they offer students the opportunity

In designing effective student interaction you will want to consider:

- **Size of Group**

- **Method for Constructing the Group**

- **Length of Time**: for the activity, for the group to stay together

- **Assignment of Roles**

for quick connection making— with peers and ideas—and they have great versatility of purpose.

There are endless methods for forming partnerships. The following list offers a few ways to get started.

1) Proximity. Efficient and effective, you simply have students connect with another student near them. Some ways to structure the exchange include:

- FAFA (Find A Friend And. . .)
- Look Behind You
- Find Someone Who. . . (you fill in a particular attribute; e.g., is wearing glasses, has a brightly colored shirt)

2) Student Selected Appointments. Prepare sheets for students to schedule appointments. For variety, you might try using a clock face, four seasons, puzzle pieces or some content-related organizer (see, for example, p. 84)

Once you have students together in pairs, you will want to challenge their thinking and engage them in purposeful tasks. Some ideas for partnered activities include:

- making predictions or generating hypotheses
- completing a stem (it might surprise you to know. . . or, one important idea in this book is . . .)
- generating questions
- creating a graphic or memory device

Learning partners can pair together as Homework Checkers. To ensure accountability, institute a Partners Report structure. Each member of the pair shares what the partner said during an exchange.

Learning Partners:

If partners are going to stay together for a week or more, have them identify an area in the room where they will always meet when partner time is called. This structuring move increases the likelihood of smooth transitions and maximizes sharing time.

Increase Accountability:

Before students meet their partner, tell them they will need to come back and report something their partner shared.

In this way, you increase individual preparation and on task behavior during partnered time.

Pairs Squared:

Once students are working well as partners, create activities for quartets—or pairs squared. By capitalizing on the relationship already established between partners, you can build students' capacity for working in larger configurations.

A Group of Ideas for Grouping

MATCHING

Create groups by distributing premade materials and directing students to find the appropriate match(es). There is no end to the creative content connections you can make.

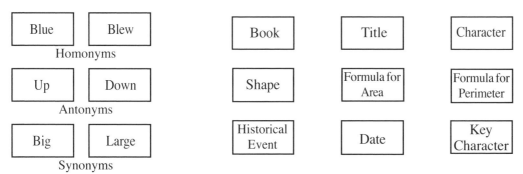

Blue	Blew
Homonyms	

Up	Down
Antonyms	

Big	Large
Synonyms	

Book	Title	Character
Shape	Formula for Area	Formula for Perimeter
Historical Event	Date	Key Character

* Create pairs by removing one of each set.

Tip:

Color code the back of each card set to make them self-correcting. That way, students can efficiently find their partners, even if they are unsure of the correct content information.

You can use a standard deck of cards to establish groups (distribute the cards and group students with same numbers, or same suits), or you can create card sets to use and reuse. Create card sets of song titles, book titles, pictures or shapes.

For Example:

Create symbol cards with a variety of colors and shapes. Try a purple square, a red circle, a yellow triangle and a green rectangle. For quartets, have students locate three people with the same shape, or three people with the same color—or they can form a group with four different shapes or colors.

If you want to assign roles within the group, you can choose one particular shape (or color) to be the recorder, another to be the checker, and so on.

COUNT-OFFS/LINE-UPS

Form groups by organizing students to line up according to some predetermined criteria. Then

a) count off and have like-numbered students form a group (for example, counting from 1 through 6 in a class of 24 students will result in groups of 4)

or

b) cluster students in the line to form the group size you require (cluster the first four students in the line to form one group, the second four to form a second group, and so on).

Add some of the following line-ups to your existing repertoire:

Sequence Line-ups:

Direct students to line-up in the order of

- Their *birthdays* (month and day)
    from January to December
- Their *street address* (house number)
    from smallest to largest
- Their *preference* for something
    from love it to can't stand it
- Their *agreement* with something
    from totally disagree to strongly agree

Estimation Line-ups:

Give students something to estimate.
Then have them line up in the order of their estimates,
from lowest to highest.
Some examples: Ask students to estimate

- The distance, in any linear measurement, from the classroom to another point in the school
- The number of lunches purchased in the school cafeteria on a given day
- A fact from an area of study (inches of rain in a geographic region, average temperature, etc.); increase/decrease in population for a particular area (New York City) as the result of a particular event (the Industrial Revolution)
- Any current factoid that would be relevant to your age group

Use a count-off grouping strategy for estimation line-ups, and then ask students to share their estimation strategies as soon as their group has formed. In this way, the grouping method can also be used to activate and engage student thinking.

TIP: *It is good practice to assign new groups a task, such as the one above, to begin as soon as the new group is assembled. The assignment should involve participation of all members but be a relatively low-risk task. In this way, the group has an immediate purpose for being together, a focus for interaction and an opportunity to build relationship.*

To increase flexibility, make card sets of six, so you can create pairs, trios, quartets or groups of five.

Be sure to mount your cards on sturdy stock and laminate to increase their durability for years of use.

Create learning activities which also serve to produce student-made materials.

For example, assign students to cutout or draw an illustration of a jungle, a forest and a domestic animal and paste each picture on an index card. Use the cards for class instruction, and then later for creating groups.

A Continuum of Interaction

As students increase their ability to learn together in pairs, you will want to increase the size of the group and the complexity and duration of the learning tasks. One way to think about designing group work is to imagine a continuum of interaction. This continuum can range from simple pairs to a full-class activity. It is difficult to lay out a specific order from most simple to most complex, because the various dimensions come together in a dynamic variety of possibilities. We encourage you to experiment with strategies described in this book. Mixing and matching a short task with a large group or a complex task with pairs will increase student success and your comfort level.

Types of Groups

Cooperatively structured groups have multiple purposes. For example, some groups will remain together over several weeks or months, while others will be together for only several minutes or hours. It is useful to make some distinctions regarding the function and purpose of the group.

We organize these distinctions into three categories; Simple Task Groups, Structured Task Groups and Home Teams.

Assigning Roles

Assigned roles structure and define an individual learner's responsibilities to the group work. Not every interactive strategy requires the use of roles. It is useful to design and assign specific roles for each group member when a group of learners has not yet developed the social skills necessary for engaging productively and cooperatively or has little experience with interactive work. Structuring roles also pays off when the group will be together for an extended period of time.

Getting Started With Roles

Roles are an example of a process scaffold. They support successful participation in a high-functioning group. Begin by defining several roles which you will use over time. Be clear about the expectations for each role; model and role-play the appropriate behaviors to be sure students can identify and produce them.

Simple Task Groups stay together for a brief period of time. Think-Pair-Share or Find a Friend And. . . (FAFA) are examples of structures suitable for Simple Task Groups.

Structured Task Groups stay together for a designated period of time and learn to function successfully as a group. Structured Task Groups might be composed of three, four or even five students. These students might stay together for a marking period, come together only during a particular subject area (such as Math or Social Studies), or remain a group only for the duration of a particular project. Structures like Jigsaws, completion of graphic organizers, or projects which require multiple steps over a period of time are suitable for Structured Task Groups.

Home Teams work together, often for the full school year, or at least a semester. The Home Team is a support group where problems are solved collaboratively and academic success is supported. Home Teams might meet twice a week or twice a day and can function as a Structured Task Group, as well. Support, both academic and emotional, is the primary function of the Structured Task.

It can be fun to create content-oriented role designations:

When studying Explorers, try:

Pilot: (recorder) keeps the log
Captain: (timekeeper) keeps the crew on course
First Mate: (provisioner) ready with materials necessary for the voyage

For Colonial America, try:
Governor: (leader) sets some guidelines
Scribe: (recorder) takes the notes
Town Crier: (checker) ensures that everyone knows what's going on

Don't introduce new roles until all class members are able to succeed with the initial ones.

Foundational roles for successful groups include; a Recorder, who keeps the record of the groups' work, a Timekeeper, who facilitates completion of the task(s) in a timely fashion and a Provisioner, who organizes the learning space and materials. You may want to add an affective role, like an Encourager, who keeps the group energized, and a high challenge role, like an Inquirer, who pushes the group to persevere, think "beyond the envelope," and challenge themselves as they engage with the task.

In Parting

Students exercise and develop skills by engaging with their peers in relevant tasks, communication, thinking and problem solving. Learning is authentic and students experience high degrees of interest and success. The following activities are a sample of the possibilities for high-impact interaction in the learning-focused classroom.

Strategies for Interactive Learning

Just Like Me!!

Just Like Me!! *is an energizing, engaging strategy for gathering information about your class. It also provides an opportunity for the learners to find out some things about each other. Just Like Me!! is especially effective early in the school year, or just after vacation breaks.*

Directions:

1. Tell students that you are going to make an "I" statement, and if it's true for them, they should stand up and say "Just like me!!"; and then look around to see who else in the group has that same thing in common with them.

2. Call out a statement, pausing between items to give students a chance to look around before sitting. Vary the items that you use to be sure that all students will have to stand up at some point, for example:

   "I have a birthday during the school year."
   "I have traveled outside of (state, city, or country) within the last two years."
   "I have a pet at home."
   "We have just had an addition to our family."
   "Both my Mom and Dad have jobs outside our home."

   Items that include preferences (favorites in music, sports, food, reading material, etc., are good choices).

NOTE: Periodically, when using content, it is important to ask students for their examples to increase accountability and determine level of knowledge.

> Just Like Me!! is a great activity to use prior to forming learning partners (see following page) because students can get some idea of others who have common interests or experiences.

Variations:

- Just Like Me!! can be used to check for content knowledge as well. You can use content-based items, such as:
   "I know a number sentence that equals 10."
   "I can find something shaped like a rectangle."
   "I can name two books by Judy Blume."
   "I can identify . . . I can name . . . I can explain . . .", etc.

- Give students "identities," (e.g., a fictional character, a member of a specific group of people, an infamous individual, historical or current, a geographical region) and have them respond to appropriate stems.

- You can use Just Like Me!! during parents night or other presentations. Some examples for parents include:

   "This is my first child attending this school."
   "I'm concerned about homework guidelines."
   "I have a special memory from (elementary/middle/high) school."

Learning Partners

Learning partners is a simple cooperative structure that is useful for quick, energizing reviews. These exchanges are especially useful when the material being presented is complex and needs to be broken into more easily digested chunks. This structure is also useful when energy lags and students need a physical lift. Checking in with a learning partner is a quick yet focused way to review and revitalize.

Directions:

1. **Students choose a learning partner.** This is done for the year, semester or unit.

2. **Teacher announces learning-partner time.** A focus question or process direction is given to define the task for the partners.

3. **Learning partners stand together.** The partners answer the question, summarize the material or react appropriately in the ways specified by the teacher's directions. This is generally a brief stand-up exchange.

4. **Students return to their seats and the lesson resumes.** You might give individual students time to write down their thoughts at this point. In other lessons, it is more appropriate to ask for oral responses to the question or task posed to the learning partners.

Establishing learning partners *can be an enjoyable and creative process. There is an endless variety of methods for establishing learning partners. One way is to use prepared forms to have students sign-up for an appointment with selected others. They then meet with their appointment partner at designated times.*

Variations:

- Assign learning partners or use a random system such as pulling names out of a basket.

- Partner's Report. Once partners have exchanged information, ask individuals to report their *partner's* response. This simple accountability move keeps students on task and increases interdependence.

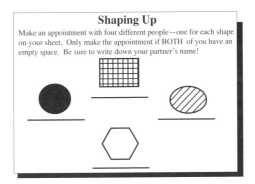

Shaping Up
Make an appointment with four different people—one for each shape on your sheet. Only make the appointment if BOTH of you have an empty space. Be sure to write down your partner's name!

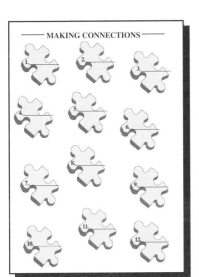

— MAKING CONNECTIONS —

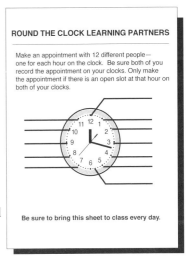

ROUND THE CLOCK LEARNING PARTNERS

Make an appointment with 12 different people—one for each hour on the clock. Be sure both of you record the appointment on your clocks. Only make the appointment if there is an open slot at that hour on both of your clocks.

Be sure to bring this sheet to class every day.

Here are some format samples for mixing and matching students. They can be used for a unit of study, for a marking period or other designated period of time, or, in an elementary classroom, for example, during one particular content area.

A See Pages 108-109

Business Cards

Business Cards *is a creative method for student introductions early in the school year, or for reinforcing facts about topics under study. The possibilities for using business cards are endless - across content areas, curriculur units and grade levels.*

Directions:

Provide each student with an index card and direct them to place the designated information in the appropriate spot on the card. Their name and descriptive characteristics make a good start. Additional information might include special interests, place of birth, hobbies, wishes, learning goals.

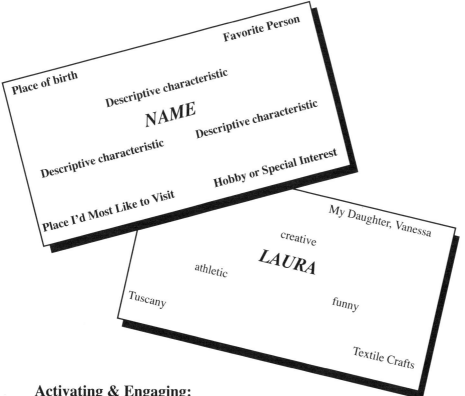

Activating & Engaging:
Use Business Cards prior to a unit of study to assess students' current understanding as well as enrich and extend their knowledge base.

Exploring & Discovering:
Establish partners and have students compare and contrast their business card content.

Organizing & Integrating:
After a unit of study, have students create Business Cards, or return to the cards they created earlier in the unit and extend the information in an essay or some other form of written expression.

Have students create business cards for:
- a famous person (historical or current);
- a fictional character;

- a geographic area (state, country, region, continent);
- an animal or plant

Paired Verbal Fluency

Paired Verbal Fluency is a strategy for getting students verbally active prior to studying or discussing a new topic. It works well to activate and engage before holding a class discussion, viewing a video, or listening to a speaker. The act of constructing language and listening to the ideas of others stimulates thinking and helps students surface knowledge about the topic at hand.

Directions:

1. Establish partners. Have each team decide which partner will be person A and which partner will be person B.

2. Assign a topic which each partner will discuss in turn. Learners should not use notes. Partners listen carefully to each other and during their own turn *do not repeat anything* already said by either person.

3. Say "Go" and A begins. After the selected time elapses say, "Switch" and B takes over. The rounds go as follows:

ROUND ONE
Teacher: *"Go"*
Person A: Talks for 60 seconds
Teacher: *"Switch"*
Person B: Talks for 60 seconds
Teacher: *"Swtich"*

ROUND TWO
Teacher: *"Go"*
Person A: Talks for 40 seconds
Teacher: *"Switch"*
Person B: Talks for 40 seconds
Teacher: *"Switch"*

ROUND THREE
Teacher: *"Go"*
Person A: Talks for 20 seconds
Teacher: *"Switch"*
Person B: Talks for 20 seconds
Teacher: *"Stop"*

NOTE: The timing of the rounds can be adjusted for the grade and experience level of the class and the content knowledge of the learners.

Variations:

- Paired Verbal Fluency (PVF) can be used after instruction as an integrating and organizing activity. After students have shared, have them independently write new thoughts, important things they want to remember, etc.

- PVF is also a good prewriting activity, or a quick review opportunity before an exam.

Think-Pair-Share

Think-Pair-Share *is a three-step discussion strategy that incorporates wait-time and cooperation with a partner. This structure was first developed by Frank Lyman at the University of Maryland. This strategy encourages participation by all class members during group discussions. Think-pair-share is applicable across all grade levels, subject matters and group sizes.*

Think-Pair-Share:

1) builds thinking time into the discussion process
2) provides time for mental rehearsal and verbal practice before sharing with the group
3) increases student engagement with the content and the class

Directions:

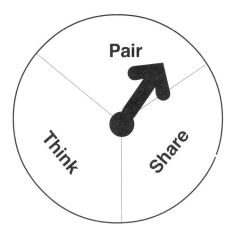

- Students listen while the teacher poses a question.
- Students are given wait-time so each can **think** of an appropriate response.
- Students are cued to **pair** with a neighbor to discuss their responses.
- Students are then invited to **share** their responses with the whole group.

Time limits can be set for each stage in the process. You can use cueing devices such as hand signals, pointers, bells or cubes to mark transition points during the cycle. When appropriate, students can be asked to write notes, or web or diagram their responses during the think and pair segments. Think-pair-share can be used several times during one class period.

Variations:

- *Think-**Write**-Pair-Share.* Have students jot down their response to the question before moving to pairs. In this way, you shift from internal engagement to an external product which focuses the interaction, and which you can use to monitor learning.

- Structure the strategy to scaffold thinking. For example, divide the class into two groups; one for an issue, the other against. During think time, direct students to "build a case" for their position. During pair time, partners explore their diverse views. Share time should produce a rich discussion from multiple perspectives.

Inter-VENN-tion

Inter-VENN-tion provides an interactive introduction to graphic organizers, as well as a way to build classroom community and social skills.

Inter-VENN-tion is a four-step strategy that follows the pattern of individual to small group work (1–4 students).

Reinforce parts of speech instruction by having students use only nouns, or only verbs in their me-maps.

1. **Individual Me-Maps**. For this step, students work on their own. Ask them to draw a circle and fill the inside with words or short phrases about themselves. They might include likes, dislikes, special experiences, favorite leisure activities, things about their family and family life, etc. Model one about yourself on a large chart paper as you describe the task.

2. **Partner-Up.** Organize the class into pairs (e.g., eye contact partners, elbow partners, or one of your favorite pairing strategies).

3. **Create a VENN.** As they explore and discover their similarities and differences, pairs create and complete a VENN diagram, placing the information in the appropriate areas. Invite students to add new information as it comes up during their discussion. Notice that they will sometimes have to create categories to organize their similarities (for example, "I like short stories" and "I like comic books" can be "We like to read").

*Pairs Squared is an efficient way to move students into larger groups (you can do Pairs Cubed, as well). It is particularly effective because some relationship has already been formed between partners, making the social skill demands of the new configuration somewhat less complex.

4. **Pairs Squared***. Each pair finds another pair and partners introduce and tell a little bit about each other. (Be sure you let the group know they will be doing this prior to forming quartets, so they can prepare).

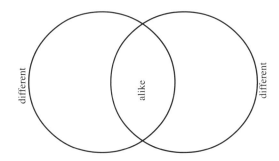

Variations:

To save class time, the individual work on the me-maps can be done at home.

- Use Inter-VENN-tion with content area information, too. For example, students can individually complete a "me-map" for a character in a story or famous person (current or historical) and then create the Venn diagram with a partner.

- This strategy is also a good way to support students' developing and sharing learning goals. Start by having students include a learning goal in their me-maps. Then, be sure to have them share their learning goals as part of the introductions in quartets. Let them know you will be collecting key goals from group members as part of the full-class sharing.

 See Pages 110-111

Three-Step Interview

The **three-step interview** *is a cooperative structure that helps students personalize their learning and listen to and appreciate the ideas and thinking of others. The structure is based on interview and listening techniques that have been modeled by the teacher. Active listening and paraphrasing by the interviewer develops understanding and empathy for the thinking of the interviewee. The content of a three-step interview is flexible. It is most often used to have students connect personal experiences to a unit of study.*

Directions:

1. Students work in pairs. One is the interviewer, the other is the interviewee. The interviewer listens actively to the comments and thoughts of the interviewee, paraphrasing key points and significant details.

2. Student pairs reverse roles, repeating the interview process.

3. Each pair joins another pair to form groups of four. Students introduce their pair partner and share what their partner had to say about the topic at hand.

Applications:

- **Activating and Engaging:** Use interview questions that surface from students' prior knowledge and experience, or cue visualization or prediction. "What do you most want to learn about this topic?" "What experiences have you had with . . .?" "When in your life would you find it useful to . . .?"

- **Organizing and Integrating:** Three-step interviews are often useful at the end of a lesson to help students make meaning of information, processes and ideas. "What did you learn from the lesson?" "What would you like to know more about?" "How will you use what you are learning?"

- **Homework Processing:** Three-step interviews can be conducted on the previous night's homework or reading. "What are some important things you remember?" "What do you have questions about?"

Story Map Trios

Story map trios *is a structured activity in which students read a piece of fiction aloud together or silently to themselves and then work collaboratively to make meaning. After reading, students work in groups of three to develop a story map to identify the key elements in the plot and create a story map.*

Each student should be assigned a specific role, as follows:

Cartographer: The cartographer captures the group's thinking and records it on the story map. If the group decides to brainstorm a number of possibilities, the cartographer should record these. However, the cartographer must wait to be sure everyone agrees before filling in the story map.

Navigator: The navigator makes sure that all members understand, agree and are comfortable with the group's decisions. The navigator guides the group's work, steering its efforts through any problems. A key function is making sure everyone is included and contributing to the thinking and final product.

Explorer: The explorer works to extend the group's thinking by exploring all avenues of thought. The explorer might ask questions like, *"Are there any other important events we haven't considered?"*, or *"What other possibilities are there?"*, or *"Where can we look for more ideas?"*

A Story Map Sample*

	Title	
Main Character(s)		**Other Character(s)**

Who?

Setting(s)

When?
Where?

Problem(s)	**Resolution(s)**

What?

Beginning	**Middle**	**End**

Why?

A **See Page 112**

* There are many varieties and methods for story mapping. Different stories often lend themselves to a particular type of structure. You may want to offer a structure to your students; or let them create one (after having some experience and modeling with several different types).

Teammates Consult

Teammates Consult *is a technique for structuring complex thinking and student collaboration into worksheet work and lab reports. Seating or grouping students in teams does not guarantee they will work cooperatively. When each team member has his or her own worksheet or lab report to fill out, animated group discussion does not always result. Yet there are times when it is useful to have every student do his or her own recording instead of using a team recorder. The trick is to structure the task so that students interact, sharing thoughts and ideas with each other rather than working on their own.*

Directions:

1. Structure groups of four students.

2. All students put their pencils or pens in the center of their team's work space. Providing a pencil holder, such as a can or beaker formalizes this step.

3. Assign the role of reader. The reader reads the first question.

4. Student teams seek the answer—from text materials, notes and by discussion.

5. The student sitting to the left of the reader checks to see that all the teammates understand and agree with the answer.

6. When there is agreement or when you call time, all teammates pick up their own pencils or pens and write the answer in their own words. There is no discussion at this point.

7. At your direction, or when they are ready, student teams move on to the next question. The checker becomes the new reader.

Source: Spencer Kagan, (1990). *Cooperative learning: Resources for teachers.* Capistrano, CA: Resources For Teachers.

Numbered Heads Together

Numbered Heads Together *is a simple and powerful cooperative structure that draws on small group interdependence and builds in individual accountability. It has a gamelike quality that is highly motivating. This structure works well for quick reviews and provides a way to easily check students' understanding of such things as content information, teacher directions, procedures and processes. Numbered Heads Together can be used for simple recall as well as for higher order questions. The time allowed for "heads-together" will vary, depending on the cognitive complexity of the thinking required by the question being processed.*

Directions:

1. Structure teams of four or five students.
2. Assign each student on the team a different number from 1 to 5.
   NOTE: If team numbers are not equal—i.e., some have four members and some have five—a simple modification is needed. All teams number to 5 whether they have four or five members. This leaves one team member with two numbers and allows all teams to answer all questions no matter what number is called.
3. Pose a question to the teams. These should be well-crafted questions that require some thought. A mix of lower and higher order questions tailored to the performance level of the students and the complexity of the material works best.
   NOTE: These should be questions on which teams can come to consensus. Questions calling for opinions can trigger disputes.
4. Heads Together. Students put their heads together and collaboratively generate an appropriate answer. Teams make sure every member knows the answer.
   NOTE: Appointing one team member to check for understanding supports team clarity.
5. Call out a number at random (see variations). All students with that number raise their hands and are called on either at random or in some designated order.

Variations:

• Using a numbered spinning wheel, die, or playing cards makes this structure more gamelike. Students appreciate and accept the fairness supplied by these random, "luck-of-the draw" strategies.
• To increase the levels of both interdependence and personal accountability, teams can be numbered as well as the individuals within them. After the head number is called, a team number can be called, with that specific person being responsible for answering for the team. Follow-up questions can then be directed to other teams by calling or "rolling" additional team numbers.
• A rehearsal stage can be added after the head number is called. The designated person in each team practices his or her answer before the team number is called. This allows each team to check for understanding and gives introverts a practice run before the public performance.
• When a student gives a partially correct answer, another person with that number can be called upon to add to the response. Another variation is to have all teams put their heads together again to check for understanding and supply the missing information.

Source: Spencer Kagan, (1990). *Cooperative learning: Resources for teachers.* Capistrano, CA: Resources For Teachers.

Walk Around Survey

Walk Around Survey is an interactive strategy that involves the full class in generating new ideas, synthesizing previously learned material or sharing present thinking and understandings. Like many other strategies designed to link and extend knowledge and experiences, it follows a pattern of 1) individual work; 2) large-group sharing; 3) small-group sharing and, in some cases 4) individual work, once again.

Directions:

1. Structure the class into small groups of 4 to 5.

2. **Individual Work.** Given the Walk Around Survey format, or worksheet and a specific topic, each student generates his or her own response for each category in the left-hand column of the page (see example, below).

3. **Full-Class Sharing.** Next, students walk around and complete their page by surveying classmates for their responses. Students briefly capture their classmates thinking in each appropriate box, as well as their name. The name provides (a) accountability and (b) potential future reference (the student can go back to the "source" for more information, or to clarify thinking). NOTE: Ask students not to collect information from their own small groups; they will have an opportunity to exchange thinking with them later on.

4. **Small-Group Processing.** When time is called (10–12 minutes, or whatever you deem appropriate), students return to their small groups. Now they share their collected information, as well as their own responses.

5. **Organize and Integrate.** Have students explore and analyze the information they have collected (look for themes, compare and contrast the items, organize into new categories). Or, you can ask students to work individually to refine their own thinking based on their new information—in writing, as a graphic organizer or outline, or perhaps as a drawing or poem.

Variations:

Walk Around Survey is applicable for all content areas and grade levels. You can vary the categories for each row to adapt for content areas, or to be grade level appropriate. For example:

> **Social Studies**—Colony Founders, Economic Products, Types of Housing
>
> **Language Arts**—Favorite Authors, Characters, Books
>
> **Mathematics**—Things that are Square, Round, Triangular

For younger students you might limit the number of boxes, or have them draw a quick picture or write a single word. If time is short, have students get a "bingo" rather than fill in the entire grid.

Walk Around Survey: Topic _____

Recollections			
My thoughts	Name_____	Name_____	Name_____
Observations			
My thoughts	Name_____	Name_____	Name_____
Insights			
My thoughts	Name_____	Name_____	Name_____

A₁ See Page 113

CHAPTER 5

FROM TEACHING-FOCUSED TO LEARNING-FOCUSED: Exploring Your Personal Pathways

*Y*ou *stand before your class, observing the levels of interaction, independence and interdependence. Some of the cooperative task groups are working on the culminating presentation for their term project while other students are working individually on self-directed learning packets. In a few minutes, you'll wander over to listen to the group discussions, making some notes about their collaborative skills as well as conference with some of the independent workers to discern their degree of completion, continued curiosity and satisfaction with the work they are doing. But for now, you watch and appreciate the classroom dynamics and student engagement.*

Learning-focused classrooms are purposefully designed and carefully cultivated. The structured environment facilitates movement. The selected materials challenge and engage. Explicit processes support collaborative thinking and learning. Teaching for connection making means that success is grounded in students' abilities to understand and apply, not simply to remember and recite. We have to identify and isolate the most important skills and ideas within the curriculum—exploring and investigating from fresh angles.

Map and Compass Work: Applying the Teaching/Learning Cycle

The foundation for Pathways to Understanding is the three-phase teaching/learning cycle introduced in Chapter Two. If we think about this cycle as the map for exploring the learning-focused classroom, then the clarity of outcomes for ourselves, our students and our classroom environment is the compass for orienteering through the complex maze of classroom life.

Focusing on the center of the framework isolates the four arenas of effective teaching decisions and behaviors; Managing, Modeling, Mediating and Monitoring. These arenas are touchstones for establishing an explicit plan for high achievement. Although each was described separately in Chapter Two, they function interactively in the learning-focused classroom.

Once the curricular context has been established, purposeful instructional planning is supported by consideration of these arenas. (See Learning-focused Teaching: A Question-Driven Approach to Planning on the following pages).

Developing a critical collaborative skill like attentive listening offers a good illustration of the reciprocal influence of monitoring and managing.

Imagine that you are in the first month of school and you want to be sure that your new fourth grade class has the appropriate skills for collaborative tasks. You do some formal and informal observing and monitoring and decide to focus on attentive listening skills. You begin by placing students in pairs, using a random card matching as a balance between directly assigning them to partners and allowing them to pick their own. You use Paired Verbal Fluency (see p. 85) on the topic of good listening as an activating and engaging strategy. Then the class discusses the importance of good listening and how it feels when someone isn't listening. Structured role-playing provides exploring and discovering time prior to a Think-Pair-Share (see p. 86) strategy for developing signs of good listening. Partners Report (see p. 83) to create a class list of these important attributes to be posted as a scaffold.

You're ready to create trios, assigning the role of observer to one of the three group members. Each group sets a listening skills goal. You use these attributes of good listening to create an observation form for group processing and self-assessment. This data will help you to determine the degree of continued

Activating & Engaging

Organizing & Integrating

- **Managing**
- **Modeling**
- **Mediating**
- **Monitoring**

Exploring & Discovering

The Pathways Learning Model guides exploration in the learning-focused classroom. Isolating the four arenas of teaching behaviors focuses decision making for student success.

focus, and whether and when to work on a new collaborative skill.

As you consider the array of choices in each decision making arena, consciousness about specific teaching behaviors increases. These considerations encourage purposeful plans connected to clear outcomes. Indicators of success can be determined, along with systems for collecting evidence of effectiveness. Sharing this information with students ensures clear expectations.

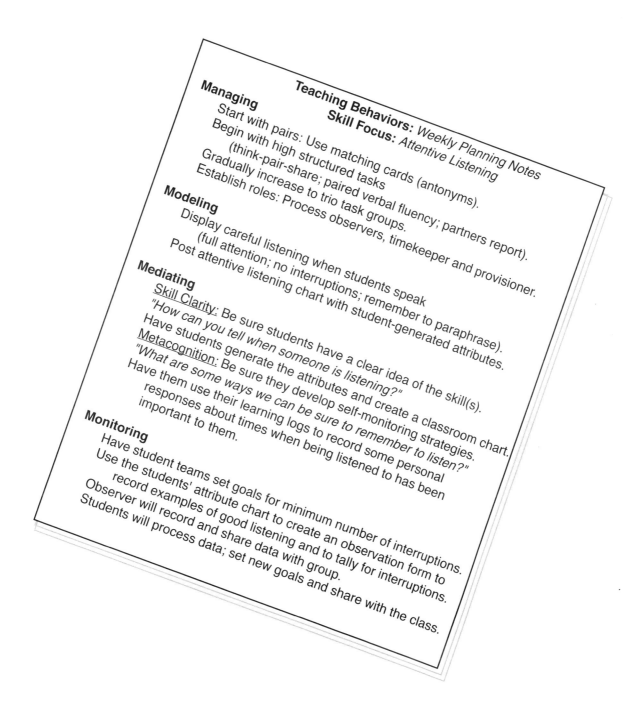

Teaching Behaviors: Weekly Planning Notes
Skill Focus: Attentive Listening

Managing
Start with pairs: Use matching cards (antonyms).
Begin with high structured tasks
    (think-pair-share; paired verbal fluency; partners report).
Gradually increase to trio task groups.
Establish roles: Process observers, timekeeper and provisioner.

Modeling
Display careful listening when students speak
    (full attention; no interruptions; remember to paraphrase).
Post attentive listening chart with student-generated attributes.

Mediating
<u>Skill Clarity:</u> Be sure students have a clear idea of the skill(s).
"How can you tell when someone is listening?"
Have students generate the attributes and create a classroom chart.
<u>Metacognition:</u> Be sure they develop self-monitoring strategies.
"What are some ways we can be sure to remember to listen?"
Have them use their learning logs to record some personal responses about times when being listened to has been important to them.

Monitoring
Have student teams set goals for minimum number of interruptions.
Use the students' attribute chart to create an observation form to record examples of good listening and to tally for interruptions.
Observer will record and share data with group.
Students will process data; set new goals and share with the class.

Learning-focused Teaching:

1. As a result of this lesson, what do I want students
   - to know?
   - to be able to do?
   - to think about?
2. How does this lesson relate to
   - this unit of study?
   - other units of study?
   - other content areas?

MANAGING

1. How should I structure resources to maximize student learning?
   - physical space
   - time
   - materials
   - group size, composition, grouping strategy

2. Where might a scaffold support student success?
   - process scaffolds?
   - product scaffolds?

MODELING

1. What procedures, skills or thinking processes will I model to increase student success?

2. What conventions of language and process should be displayed to support student learning?

MEDIATING

1. What major connections do I want to make explicit during this lesson?
   - backtracking (to previous learning and experiences)
   - foreshadowing (to future learning opportunities)
   - transferring (to other content and contexts)

2. What thinking strategies can be surfaced and developed during this lesson?
   - cognitive (thinking processes and skills)
   - metacognitive (processing the mental operations and learning habits employed during this lesson)

A Question-Driven Approach to Planning

MONITORING

1. To what do I need to pay attention during this lesson?
    - About my students
        student engagement
            (with the materials; with each other)
        student understanding
            (about major ideas and content specific information)
        student development
            (of cognitive and metacognitive processes)

    - For me
        instructional decisions
            (use of time, clarity of directions,
                grouping strategies, etc.)
        questions and response behaviors
            (pausing, paraphrasing, inquiring, calling-upon
                patterns)
        nonverbals
            (intonation, facial expression, gestures, location
                and movement in room)

2. How will I monitor student and group development?
    - What information will be collected?
    - How will it be gathered (e.g., observation form,
        anecdotal records, student products)?

3. What processing strategies will we use to determine success
    and identify continued learning?
    - How will students and groups receive feedback?
    - What reflection process will we use for student and
        group self-assessment?

4. What will be the indicators of success in this lesson?
    - Process
    - Product

5. How will I communicate and clarify these criteria with
    students before we begin?

From Teaching-centered to Learning-focused: Some Traveling Tips

New learning is fragile. With the best intentions, it is still difficult to keep from reverting to old habits when things are hectic or stressful or when time is short. We offer some practical ideas to sustain your new understandings and commitment to learning-focused practice.

Markers and Milestones

As you start out, establish milestones for yourself. Just as you would encourage your students to do, set learning goals and identify strategies for achieving success. Choose from among the various ideas in this volume those that will be most useful to you. Start with small, realistic goals. Once these have been achieved, continue to purposefully expand your repertoire.

Here are some ideas for scaffolding your own learning:

1. **Make a date for learning**

   Place markers on specific days in your planbook or calendar. Use a colorful sticky dot, or other symbol that says, "I will try a new instructional strategy today."

   Or, setup a systematic process for skill development. For example, you might decide that on Mondays you will practice paraphrase, on Wednesdays you'll use a new grouping strategy and on Fridays you'll choose an interactive strategy that you haven't yet tried.

2. **Monitor your progress**

   Use the strategy log at the end of this chapter to keep a record of the things you try and what you are learning, or buy a blank book that you'll enjoy using to keep track of your progress.

3. **Ring of strategies**

   To keep the Pathways strategies accessible, write the directions for those that interest you on large index cards. Keep the cards on a binder ring in your desk or other convenient area. When you're ready to try something new, pull out the ring and flip through the ideas. When you've tried one, note how you used it on the back, so you can either repeat it or vary it for the next time.

   Brainstorm & Pass
   1. Establish small groups and set ground rules for brainstorming

   Brainstorm & Pass

   Oct. 15: Used as an activating & engaging strategy for our unit on state history. Had to reinforce the rules several times with two groups. Next time, I'll reduce

   Oct. 28: Second try went better. I noticed some of the quieter kids being involved, and I was especially pleased to

4. **Teach, post, reinforce, remove**

   Target a strategy that you expect to use frequently and make a directions chart for posting in the classroom. Use the chart for reference, until the strategy becomes part of your (and your students) repertoire. Then move it to another area in the room (or put it away) and continue the process with new strategies.

Gearing Up

Just as any traveler prepares and provisions carefully for their sojourns, you will want to gear up thoughtfully for your explorations. The blackline masters and other resources in this chapter are designed to "fill your backpack" with some initial supplies. We know that you will add, delete, adjust and create as you gain experience and confidence.

There are potential challenges and hazards ahead. These may include feelings of awkwardness in trying on new ways to operate in the classroom, the discomfort of uncovering the content rather than covering it, the stretch of shifting from activity planning to outcome planning and the messiness of offering choice and self-direction to the students.

There is also great adventure. While you may experience the vulnerability of co-learning, no longer dispensing knowledge, but gathering and creating it with your students, you will also enjoy the freedom of this approach.

Although this book provides ideas, information and support materials, in essence, your most important resource is your own willingness to experiment, your courage to take risks and your commitment to continual learning for yourself and your students.

> . . . your most important resource is your own willingness to experiment, your courage to take risks and your commitment to continual learning for yourself and your students.

Blackline Masters
and Other
Resources

Four BOX SYNECTICS

+-------------------+-------------------+
+-------------------+-------------------+
+-------------------+-------------------+

_____ is

like a(n)_____

because . . .

See Chapter 2: Page 22

NORMS FOR BRAINSTORMING

Flexibility and fluidity of thinking is encouraged.

Lots of ideas is the goal; all ideas are recorded.

Open acceptance of all ideas is necessary.

Withhold all judgment (both criticism and praise)

See Chapter 2: Page 25

+1

3 :•••

2 :••

1 :•

See Chapter 2: Page 43

5 - 3 - 1

1. On your own, write down five words:

2. Our three words are:

3. Our group's word is:

HERE'S WHAT!	SO WHAT?	NOW WHAT?

See Chapter 2: Page 40

See Chapter 2: Page 36

Name _____

ROUND THE CLOCK LEARNING PARTNERS

Make an appointment with 12 different people—one for each hour on the clock.
Be sure both of you record the appointment on your clocks.
Only make the appointment if there is an open slot at that hour on both of your
clocks.

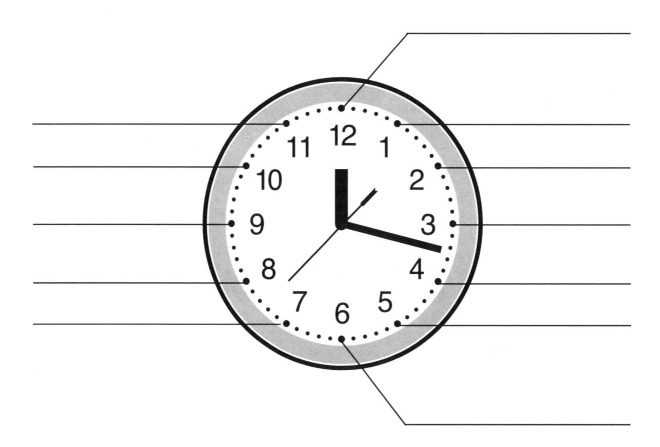

Be sure to bring this sheet to class every day.

See Chapter 4: Page 83

———— MAKING CONNECTIONS ————

1. _____

2. _____

3. _____

4. _____

5. _____

6. _____

7. _____

8. _____

9. _____

10. _____

11. _____

12. _____

INTER - VENN - TION

My learning goal. . . .

Name _____

See Chapter 4: Page 87

INTER - VENN - TION

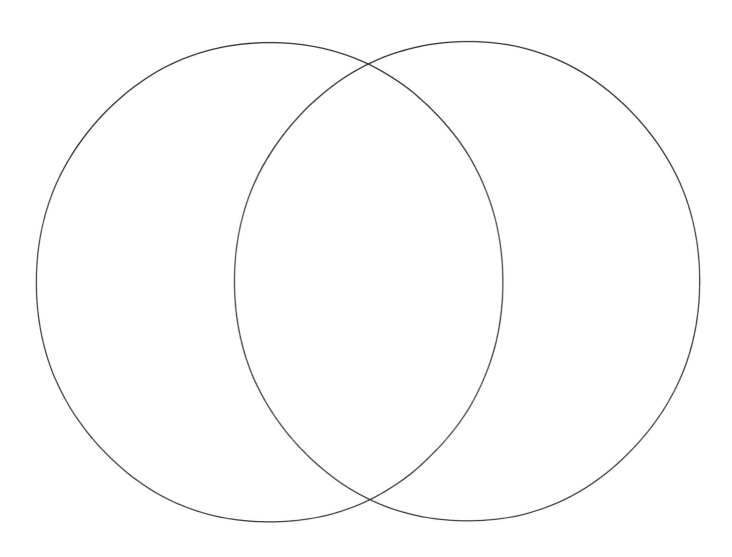

Share your learning goals here:

Names _____ **&** _____

Cartographer:

The cartographer records the group's thinking, first on a brainstormed list - - then on the story map.

REMEMBER to include each group member's ideas on the list, even if you don't agree. Be sure to wait until everyone agrees before recording on the story map.

Navigator:

The navigator guides the group's work, steering through problems toward a successful conclusion, making sure that all members understand, agree and are comfortable with the group's decisions.

Ask individual group members to give examples and to summarize the group's work. Pay special attention to quiet members; be sure everyone is included and contributing to the thinking and final product.

Explorer:

The explorer extends the group's thinking by exploring all avenues of thought. It is important to generate lots of ideas before deciding on one for the story map.

Ask questions like, "Are there any other important events we haven't considered?", or "What other possibilities are there?" or "Where can we look for more ideas?"

Walk Around Survey

Topic _____

_____

_____

_____

STRATEGY USE LOG

Chapter 2

Date   Strategy

☐
☐
☐
☐
☐
☐
☐
☐
☐
☐
☐
☐
☐
☐
☐
☐
☐
☐
☐
☐
☐
☐
☐
☐

Chapter 3

Date   Strategy

☐
☐
☐
☐
☐
☐
☐
☐
☐
☐
☐
☐
☐
☐
☐
☐
☐
☐
☐
☐
☐
☐
☐
☐

Chapter 4

Date   Strategy

☐
☐
☐
☐
☐
☐
☐
☐
☐
☐
☐
☐
☐
☐
☐
☐
☐
☐
☐
☐
☐
☐
☐

STRATEGY USE LOG

Chapter 2

Date	Strategy
☐	
☐	
☐	
☐	
☐	
☐	
☐	
☐	
☐	
☐	
☐	
☐	
☐	
☐	
☐	
☐	
☐	
☐	
☐	
☐	

Chapter 3

Date	Strategy
☐	
☐	
☐	
☐	
☐	
☐	
☐	
☐	
☐	
☐	
☐	
☐	
☐	
☐	
☐	
☐	
☐	
☐	
☐	
☐	

Chapter 4

Date	Strategy
☐	
☐	
☐	
☐	
☐	
☐	
☐	
☐	
☐	
☐	
☐	
☐	
☐	
☐	
☐	
☐	
☐	
☐	
☐	
☐	

A Learner's Log

. . . musings . . . insights . . . thoughts . . . discoveries . . . . implications . . . wonderings . . . intrigues . . . questions . . . reflections . . . notes . . . ideas . . .

116

A Learner's Log

*. . . musings . . . insights . . . thoughts . . . discoveries . . . . implications . . .
wonderings . . . intrigues . . . questions . . . reflections . . . notes . . . ideas . . .*

A LEARNER'S LOG

*. . . musings . . . insights . . . thoughts . . . discoveries . . . implications . . .
wonderings . . . intrigues . . . questions . . . reflections . . . notes . . . ideas . . .*

References

Selected Bibliography and References

America 2000: An education strategy. Washington, DC: U. S. Department of Education.

Anderson, J. (1987). Skill acquisition: Compilation of weak-method problem solutions. *Psychological Review, 94:* 192–210.

Anderson, R., Hiebert, E., Scott, J. & Wilkinson, A. (1985). *Becoming a nation of readers: The report of the commission on reading.* Urbana, IL: University of Illinois.

Barbe, W. & Swassing, R. H. (1979). *Teaching through modality strengths: Concepts and practices.* Columbus, OH: Zaner-Bloser.

Baron, J. (1986). *Evaluating thinking skills in the classroom.* In Baron, J.B. & Sternberg, R., (Eds.). Teaching thinking skills. New York: W. H. Freeman & Co.

Bellanca, J. & Fogarty, R. (1990). *Blueprints for thinking in the cooperative classroom.* Palantine, IL: Skylight Publications.

Beyer, B. (1987). *Practical strategies for the teaching of thinking.* Boston: Allyn & Bacon.

Black, H. & Black, S. (1990). *Organizing thinking: Graphic organizers.* Pacific Grove, CA: Midwest Publications.

Borkowski, J. G., Carr, M., Rellinger, E., & Pressley, M. (1990). Self-regulated cognition: Interdependence of metacognition, attributions, and self-esteem. In Jones, B. F. & Idol, L. (Eds.). *Dimensions of thinking and cognitive instruction.* Hillsdale, NJ: Lawrence Erlbaum Associates.

Bransford, J., Sherwood, R., Vye, N., & Rieser, J. (1986). Teaching thinking and problem solving. *American Psychologist, 41:* 1078–1089.

Bransford, J.D. Brown, A. & Cocking, R. (1999). *How people learn: Brain, mind, experience and school.* Washington, D.C.: National Academy Press

Brown, A. (1980). Metacognitive development and reading. In Spiro, R., Bruce, B. & Brewer, W. (Eds.). *Theoretical issues in reading comprehension.* Hillsdale, NJ: Lawrence Erlbaum Associates.

Brown, A. L., Campione, J. C., & Day, J. D. (1981). Learning to learn: On training students to learn from text. *Educational Researcher, 10:* 14–21.

Brown, A., Bransford, J., Ferrarra, R. & Campione, J. (1983). Learning, remembering, and understanding. In Flavell, J. & Markham, E. (Eds.). *Handbook of child psychology, Vol. 3.* New York: John Wiley & Sons.

Chi, M., Glaser, R. & Farr, M. (1988). *The nature of expertise.* Hillsdale, NJ: Lawrence Erlbaum Associates.

Chittenden, E. (1991). *Authentic assessment, evaluation and documentation of student performance.* In Perrone, V., Ed. Expanding student assessment. Alexandria, VA: ASCD.

Costa, A. (1985) *Teaching for intelligent behaviors.* Orangevale, CA: Search Models Unlimited.

Costa, A. (1991a). The principal's role in enhancing thinking. In Costa, A. (Ed.). *Developing minds: A resource book for teaching thinking.* Alexandria, VA: ASCD.

Costa, A., Ed. (1991b) *Developing minds: A resource book for teaching thinking.* Alexandria, VA: Association for Supervision and Curriculum Development.

Costa, A. & Lowery, L. (1989). *Techniques for teaching thinking.* Pacific Grove, CA: Midwest Publications.

Costa, A. & Marzano, R. (1991). Teaching the language of thinking. In Costa, A. (Ed.). *Developing minds: A resource book for teaching thinking.* Alexandria, VA: Association for Supervision and Curriculum Development.

deBono, E. (1970). *Lateral thinking: Creativity step by step.* New York: Harper & Row.

Dillon, R. & Sternberg, R. (1986). *Cognition and instruction.* New York: Academic Press.

Edmonds, R. (1982). Programs of school improvement: An overview. *Educational Leadership, 40*: 4–11.

Eisner, E. (1988). The ecology of school improvement. *Educational Leadership, 45:* 24–29.

Feldman, R. D. What are thinking skills and how do you teach them?, *Instructor and Teacher,* April 1986: 34–39.

Feuerstein, R. (1980). *Instrumental enrichment.* Baltimore, MD: University Press.

Feathers, Karen M. (1993). *Infotext, reading and learning.* Markham, Ontario: Pippen Publishing Ltd.

Fulwiler, T. (Ed.). (1987). *The journal book.* Portsmouth, NH: Boynton/Cook - Heinemann.

Freedman, R., & Harris, L. (1990). *Connections: Science by writing.* Carmichael CA: Serin House Publishers.

Garner, R. (1987). *Metacogniton and reading comprehension.* Norwood, NJ: Abex.

Garner, R. (1990). When children and adults do not use learning strategies: Toward a theory of settings. *Review of Educational Research, 60*(4): 517–530.

Glaser, R. (1976). Components of a psychology of instruction: Toward a science of design. *Review of Educational Research, 46* (1): 1–24.

Graves, D. (1989). *Investigate nonfiction.* Portsmouth, NH: Heinemann Educational Books.

Graves, M. & Graves, B. (1994). *Scaffolding reading experiences.* Norwood, MA: Christopher-Gordon.

Grinder, M. (1993). *EnVoy: Your Personal guide to classroom management.* Battle Ground, WA: Michael Grinder & Associates.

Hampden-Turner, C. (1981). *Maps of the mind: Charts and concepts of the mind and its labyrinths.* New York: MacMillan.

Heimlich, J. E. & Pittelman, S. (1986). *Semantic mapping: Classroom applications.* Newark, DE: International Reading Association.

Hunt, J. (1972). *Human intelligence.* New Brunswick, NJ: Dutton.

Hyerle, D. (1990). *Designs for thinking connectively.* Cary, NC: Innovative Sciences.

Hyerle, D. (1991). Expand your thinking. In Costa, A. (Ed.). *Developing minds: A resource book for teaching thinking.* Alexandria, VA: Association for Supervision and Curriculum Development.

Hyerle, D. & Goodman, S. (1989). *Expand your thinking.* Cary, NC: Innovative Sciences.

Iran-Nejad, A., McKeachie, W. & Berliner, D. (1990) The multisource nature of learning: An introduction. *Review of Educational Research, 60*(4): 509–513.

Irvin, J. L. (1990). *Reading and the middle school student: Strategies to enhance literacy.* Boston: Allyn and Bacon.

Jones, B., Palinscar, A., Ogle, D. & Carr, E. (1987). *Strategic teaching and learning: Cognitive instruction in the content areas.* Alexandria, VA: Association for Supervision and Curriculum Development.

Joyce, B. & Weil, M. (1986). *Models of teaching.* Englewood Cliffs, NJ: Prentice-Hall.

Kagan, S. (1990). *Cooperative learning: Resources for teachers.* Capistrano, CA: Resources For Teachers.

Khatena, J. (1984). *Imagery and creative imagination.* Buffalo, NY: Bearly Limited.

Laborde, G. Z. (1983). *Influencing with integrity.* Palo Alto: Syntony Publishing.

Leinhardt, G. (1991). What research on learning tells us about teaching. *Educational Leadership, 49* (7): 20–25.

Lipton, L. & Hubble, D. (1997). *More than 50 ways to learner-centered literacy.* Palantine IL: Skylight Press.

Markova, D. (1992). *The art of the possible: A compassionate approach to understanding the way people think, learn and communicate.* Emeryville, CA: Conari Press.

Margulies, N. (1991). *Mapping inner space: Learning and teaching mind mapping,* Tuscon, AZ: Zephyr Press.

Marzano, R., Brandt, R., Hughes, C., Jones, B., Presseisen, B., Rankin, C. & Suthor, C. (1988). *Dimensions of thinking: A framework for curriculum and instruction.* Alexandria, VA: Association for Supervision and Curriculum Development.

Mayer, W. & Mayer, B. (1989). *The art of science writing.* New York: Teachers and Writers' Collaborative.

McTighe, J. (1987). Teaching for thinking, of thinking, and about thinking. In Heiman & Somainko (Eds.). *Thinking skills instruction: Concepts and techniques.* Washington, DC: National Education Assocation.

McTighe, J. & Lyman, F. (1991a). Cueing thinking in the classroom: The promise of theory embedded tools. In Costa, A. (Ed.). *Developing minds: A resource book for teaching thinking.* Alexandria, VA: Association for Supervision and Curriculum Development.

McTighe, J. & Lyman, F. (1991b). Mind tools for matters of the mind. In Costa, Bellanca, & Fogarty (Eds). *If minds matter: A foreword to the future.* Palantine, IL: Skylight Press: 70–100.

Moore, D., Readence, J. & Rickerman, R. (1989). *Prereading activities for content area reading and learning,* 2nd ed., Newark DE: International Reading Association.

Novak, J. D. & Gowan, D. B. (1984). *Learning how to learn.* Cambridge: Cambridge University Press.

Ornstein, R. & Thompson, R. (1984). *The amazing brain.* Boston: Houghton Mifflin.

Paris, S., Lipson, M. & Wixson. K. (1983). Becoming a strategic reader. *Contemporary Educational Psychology, 8*: 293–316.

Pearson, P. D. & Dole, J. (1987). Explicit comprehension instruction: A review of research and a new conceptualization of instruction. *Elementary School Journal, 88*(2). Chicago: The University of Chicago.

People for the American Way. (1989). *Democracy's next generation: A study of youth and teachers.* Washington, D.C.: People for the American Way.

Perkins, D. (1986a). *Knowledge as design.* Hillsdale, NJ: Lawrence Erlbaum Associates.

Perkins, D. (1986b). Thinking frames. *Educational Leadership, 43* (8): 4–10.

Perkins, D. & Salomon, G. (1988). Teaching for transfer. *Educational Leadership, 46* (1): 22–32.

Presseisen, B. (1987). *Thinking skills throughout the curriculum.* Bloomington, IN: Pi Lambda Theta, Inc.

Raths, L., Wasserman, S., Jonas, A., & Rothstein, A. (1986). *Teaching for thinking: Theory, strategies, & activities for the classroom.* New York: Teachers College Press.

Resnick, L. (1984). Cognitive science as educational research: Why we need it now. In National Academy of Education. *Improving education: Perspective on educational research.* Pittsburgh, PA: University of Pittsburgh, Learning and Development Center.

Resnick, L. (1989). *Toward the thinking curriculum: Current cognitive research.* Alexandria, VA: Association for Supervision and Curriculum Development.

Rowe, M. (1983). Getting chemistry off the killer course list. *Journal of Chemical Education, 60* (11): 954–956.

Rowe, M. (1986). Wait time: Slowing down may be a way of speeding up! *Journal of Teacher Education,* Jan-Feb: 43–49.

Santa, C. M . & Alvermann, D. (Eds.). (1991). *Science learning, processes and applications.* Newark, DE: International Reading Association.

Schon, D. (1983). *The reflective practitioner: How professionals think in action.* New York: Basic Books.

Scott, J., Ed. (1993). *Science and language links.* Portsmouth, NH: Heinemann Educational Books.

Schuell, T. (1986). Individual differences: Changing concepts in research and practice. *American Journal of Education, 94*: 356–377.

Schuell, T. (1990). Phases of meaningful learning. *Review of Educational Research, 60*(4): 530–547.

Shepard, L. (1989). Why we need better assessments. *Educational Leadership, 46*(7). Alexandria, VA: Association for Supervision and Curriculum Development.

Schwartz, R. & Perkins, D. (1989). *Teaching thinking: Issues and approaches.* Pacific Grove, CA: Midwest Publications.

Sommer, R. (1978). *The mind's eye: Imagery in everyday life.* Palo Alto: Dale Seymour.

Sternberg, R. (1984). Towards a triarchic theory of human intelligence. *Behavioral and brain sciences, 7*: 269–315.

Sternberg, R. & Wagner, R. (1982). *Understanding intelligence: What's in it for education.* Paper submitted to the National Commission on Excellence in Education.

Strong, R. W., Hanson, J. R. & Silver, H. (1986). *Questioning styles and strategies: Procedures for increasing the depth of student thinking.* Moorestown, NJ: Hanson Silver Strong Associates, Inc.

Taba, H. (1962). *Curriculum development.* New York: Harcourt, Brace & World.

Thelen, Judith N. (1984). *Improving reading in science.* Newark, DE: International Reading Association.

Vygotsky, L. S. (1962). *Thought and language.* Cambridge, MA: MIT Press.

Wang, M. C., Haertel, G. & Walberg, H. (1993). What helps students learn? *Educational Leadership,* Alexandria, VA: Association for Supervision and Curriculum Development.

Weiner, B. (1985). An attributional theory of achievement and emotion. *Psychological Review, 92:* 548–573.

Wellman, B. & Lipton, L. (1991). *Making meaning: Linking primary science and literature.* Presentation at the National Conference Association for Supervision and Curriculum Development. San Francisco, CA.

Whimbey, A. (1989). *Analytic reading and reasoning.* Cary, NC: Innovative Sciences, Inc.

Winograd, P. (1989). Improving basal reading instruction: Beyond the carrot and the stick. *Theory Into Practice, 28*(4): 240–247.

Wood, K. D., Lapp, D. & Flood, J. (1992). *Guiding readers through text: A review of study guides,* Newark, DE: International Reading Association.

Wood, P., Bruner, J. & Ross, G. (1976). The role of tutoring in problem solving. *Journal of Child Psychology and Psychiatry, 17:* 89–100.

INDEX

Additional Learning Opportunities
Putting Theory into Practice in Your Schools

Seminars • Keynotes • Consulting Services

MiraVia provides learning-focused professional development programs and services
that present practical strategies, useful resources and innovative ideas
for thoughtful educators grappling with critical professional issues.

Developing Learning-Focused Relationships

Target Audience: Teacher mentors, instructional and content coaches, curriculum specialists and instructional supervisors

Explore the essential concepts, templates and mediational tools for developing
effective,learning-focused relationships between growth-oriented educators.

Workshops and seminars include
- Mentoring Matters: A Practical Guide to Learning-Focused Relationships
- Learning-Focused Relationships: Coaching, Collaborating and Consulting for Professional Excellence
- Learning-Focused Supervision: Calibrating Professional Excellence

Building Professional Community

Target Audience: School and district leaders, site and district teams, facilitators and group developers

Learn critical skills for developing collaborative school cultures that focus on the learning
needs of students and the adults who serve them.

Workshops and seminars include
- Data-Driven Dialogue: Facilitating Collaborative Inquiry
- Leading Groups: Framing, Presenting, Collaborating and Facilitating
- Learning-Focused Presentations
- The Facilitator's Toolkit: Balancing Task, Process and Relationship
- Teacher to Teacher: Working Collaboratively for Student Success

Creating Learning-Focused Classrooms and Schools

Target Audience: Beginning and experienced classroom teachers, staff developers, instructional leaders

Discover the bridge between current learning theory and effective classroom practice.
Our research-based and classroom-tested Pathways Learning Model offers a coherent
framework for organizing lessons and units of study.

Workshops and seminars include
- Pathways to Understanding: Patterns and Practices in the Learning-Focused Classroom
- Pathways to Literacy: Reading and Writing in the Content Areas
- Getting Started, Getting Smarter: Practical Tools for Beginning Teachers
- Thinking to Learn, Learning to Think

MiraVia offers seminars in a variety of formats for customized programs

Awareness Sessions: 1-2 days   Foundation Seminars: 4-6 days   Advanced Seminars: 2-4 days

FOR INFORMATION
On Professional Development

Laura Lipton   or   Bruce Wellman
lelipton@miravia.com   bwellman@miravia.com
860-354-4543   802-257-4892

About Our Products

e-mail info@miravia.com
phone 781-316-8484
fax 781-998-0298

or visit our website www.miravia.com

MiraVia ® *The Road To Learning*
LLC www.miravia.com

Based on our book of the same title

mira (L.)[MIR-â]: wonderful/amazing   via (L.)[VE-â]: way or road

IN 1596, the German astronomer Fabricus saw a third magnitude star in the constellation Cetus, the Whale. As they continued to observe it over the next century, astronomers became aware of its unusual fluctuations, now brighter, now fading, and honored it with the name Mira, the Wonderful.

As a partnership dedicated to continued development for professionals, we connect the constancy of presence and fluctuating brightness with the learning process. We believe that learning means working through the temporary dullness of not knowing, while pursuing the brilliance of new understanding. Our name, and our philosophy, combines this wonder of learning, Mira, with Via, or the road. Our publications, products and seminars offer pathways to professional insight and growth.